REWIRED

POWER UP YOUR

PERFORMANCE, RELATIONSHIPS, AND PURPOSE

JOEL LANDI

Acknowledgements

Thanks to my wife, Julie, and our daughters, Natasha and Misha. Your love makes me complete.

A special thanks to my father and his wife, Hope. Their wit, creativity, and sense of adventure continue to inspire us.

Thanks to my friends Steve Johnson, 1 MC; Steve Morici, Bob Scholten, Howard Lynggard, Reese and Mary Kay Neyland, Dan Klier, Brent Hammond, Michael Herzog (Berlin), Steve Radenbaugh, Eric Schick, Allen Berg, David Anthony, Dana Mech, Joseph Yacoe, Peter Brennen, Lisa Lew, and Brandi Kamenar. All of you have played pivotal roles in the journey. Without all of you, this wouldn't have been possible.*

I also want to thank Rob Kosberg for his friendship and guidance as my publisher.

Cover photographer: Ray Christian

TABLE OF CONTENTS

Introduction

The Hillary Step

"Quitting is a response that follows the belief that whatever you do doesn't matter."

– Arnold Schwarzenegger

Our ex-governor from California couldn't have been more spot-on: Quitting is something that follows a belief. When we give up on someone or something that's important to us, it's usually tied to a negative belief about ourselves or a particular person or thing.

Limiting Beliefs

It's not unusual for people to invest months, sometimes even years, in a project, career or relationship and still not succeed. They sought sound advice, did many things right, but in the end, fell short of achieving their desired objective.

Whether we're building a business, advancing a relationship or working to achieve and reach a milestone, the beliefs we've inherited and come to count on, can— without us realizing why-- form obstacles to our goals. But we can rewire our beliefs; we can re-wire our views on the foundational topics of achievement, power, wealth, sex and self-worth. Then we can experience a true paradigm shift, break free from a debilitating mindset, and move onto to greater things. The challenging part is identifying which belief is limiting.

The Privileged Few

How is it that some are able to make it? They survive the near divorce only to write a bestselling book on marriage and live happily ever after. They pull the equity out of their personal home, borrow obscene amounts of money from family and friends, and navigate a startup company to a seven-figure salary. How?

What separates the successful from the unsuccessful? It's their ability to push past limiting beliefs, the thoughts that reside in the subconscious mind that say there is an insurmountable barrier to success. Everyone feels the barriers, and most give up. But some overcome this monumental hurdle and go on to claim their prize. In my coaching practice, I refer to this as the Hillary Step.

The Hillary Step

The Hillary Step is a small but very difficult rock face located within 300 feet of the summit of the world's highest mountain, Mount Everest. At an elevation of 29,029 feet, Mount Everest is so high that the jet stream can hit it, subjecting climbers to face winds that can exceed 200 mph. When the weather shifts, it can dump 10 feet of snow in a matter of hours. Most expeditions

require supplemental oxygen above 26,000 feet.[1]

The New Zealander Edmund Hillary and the Nepali Sherpa climber from Darjeeling, India, Tenzing Norgay, were the first to ascend Mount Everest successfully. They reached the summit at 11:30 am local time on May 29, 1953, via the south route. Nearing the end of their epic climb, Hillary and Norgay encountered an imposing 39-foot sheer rock face, which would later be named the Hillary Step in honor of Sir Edmund.[2]

The Hillary Step has frequently become a bottleneck for climbers. It forces climbers to wait significant amounts

1. Mount Everest (n.d.) Retrieved May 5, 2015, from http://en.wikipedia.org/wiki/Mount_Everest

2. Mount Everest (n.d.) Retrieved May 5, 2015, from http://en.wikipedia.org/wiki/Mount_Everest

of time for their turn on the ropes and exposing them to a much greater risk for altitude sickness, physiological depletion, and death.[3]

A Potent Metaphor

With any great undertaking, there is often a seemingly insurmountable obstacle that we have to overcome before we can reach our goal. In the realm of personal development, the Hillary Step symbolizes an obstacle that we've created in our mind. It is a mental barrier that can appear to be insurmountable, or it can even go undetected.

People might not realize the lingering thoughts in their subconscious that sabotages them from going forward and claiming their victory. However, with the right Sherpa, in this case, the coaching relationship, you can navigate the obstacle, secure your footing, and get to the summit.

Once above the Hillary Step, it is comparatively easy to climb to the top on moderately angled snow slopes to the summit. The same holds true for the coaching relationship. The Hillary Step is the place where we remove the limiting belief and shift our paradigm. Once this happens, we are reenergized to take the summit.

---

3. Everest 2013: Ladder on the Hillary Step? A Bad Idea. (2013, May 28). Retrieved May 5, 2015, from http://www.alanarnette.com/blog/2013/05/28/everest-2013-ladder-on-the-hillary-step-a-bad-idea/

Moving past Your Hillary Step

Are you stuck in your career? Do you want to be promoted but are fearful of leading meetings or public speaking? Are you exhausted from struggling to balance work and life? Do you want to date someone or commit to a serious relationship but are afraid to fail? Do you want to do what you have threatened to do but have not prepared for properly? Are you a romantic who just wants "to boldly go where no man or woman has gone before"? Do you want to start over? *Then unravel your limiting beliefs, change your paradigm, and move past your Hillary Step.*

Chapter takeaway: Limiting beliefs are self-sabotaging thoughts that derail us from great achievement and personal fulfillment. A great coaching partner can help you move past your Hillary Step – the insurmountable mental barrier that stands between you and your goal. Once above the Hillary Step, your summit is attainable.

Our Resistance to Change

Chapter 1

*"Philosophers have only interpreted the world
in various ways. The point, however, is to change it."*

– Karl Marx

In the introduction, we touched on the power of the mind and the concept of limiting beliefs. Before we revisit the topic of limiting beliefs, let us establish a fundamental distinction between the conscious and the subconscious mind.

The Conscious and the Subconscious Mind

Rational, critical thinking takes place in the conscious mind. Values, beliefs, intuition, and imagination take place in the subconscious mind. It takes a more intentional effort to work on the subconscious mind. In addition to psychological counseling, there is now a host of industry standards tests and tools available, and competent practitioners, such as coaches, can use these to understand the subconscious mind and its role to improve performance and behavior.

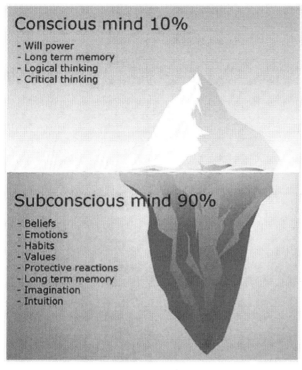

Conscious mind 10%
- Will power
- Long term memory
- Logical thinking
- Critical thinking

Subconscious mind 90%
- Beliefs
- Emotions
- Habits
- Values
- Protective reactions
- Long term memory
- Imagination
- Intuition

Last year, I got a traffic ticket for rolling through a stop sign. My conscious mind knows it's wrong to roll through a stop sign. However, there are other thought streams in the subconscious mind that drive behavior. In this situation, the subconscious mind could be telling me, "You're not getting any younger, Joel – and every second counts – so step on it." Our subconscious mind drives both wanted and unwanted behavior. So how do we change the subconscious thinking that drives unwanted behavior?

According to Athena Staik, Ph.D., the solution is "to make conscious the subconscious" by becoming aware (conscious) of unwanted *perceptions* held in the subconscious mind. Once we become aware of the thoughts that drive unwanted behavior, we can begin to change them.[1]

---

1. Staik, A. (n.d.). Three Laws of Change – How to Influence Your Subconscious to Manage the Energies of Your Heart. Retrieved May 5, 2015, from http://blogs.psychcentral.com/relationships/2011/03/the-laws-of-change-and-the-subconscious-mind/

Herein lies the rub: Changing what can be obvious to others takes more involvement than we understand at times. Sometimes, even a plan with clear goals and accountability won't do the trick. We have to deal with the root of the issue: a flawed or limiting belief. Not dealing with the root is why diets, marriages, and careers fail. But here is the good news: Dr. Staik reminds us that we can alter subconscious thinking with a competent thinking partner and a blueprint to address limitations of the subconscious mind.

The solution to feeling stuck, isolated, or hopeless is to remove our limiting beliefs. Finally, relief has arrived, and the sun begins to shine again in our time of darkness.

Why We Get Stuck

What is our resistance to change? It is our limiting beliefs held in the subconscious mind that sabotage what we want. We don't evolve and conquer new frontiers by interpreting facts and explaining reasons for unwanted behaviors and outcomes, but by finding the mechanism to change them. And that's what *Rewired* is all about.

The secret weapon to changing patterns of thinking, habits, and even outcomes is attacking the obstacle at the appropriate place: our limiting belief. By identifying the limiting belief as the root of the resistance to change, we break free from the static thinking that holds us captive. This opens the door to new frontiers and great gains. As Karl Marx tells us above, let's not talk about change. Let's do it.

Revisiting Limiting Beliefs

Now let's consider some common limiting beliefs that we can be duped into accepting as true and permanent. If this belief goes uncontested, it has a sabotaging influence that restricts our potential and leaves us captive to unwanted negative emotions.

A few common examples of limiting beliefs are:

- "I'm not experienced enough."
- "I wasn't blessed with that skill set."
- "I'm too old / too young to be thinking like this."
- "I just don't have the contacts, resources, or energy."
- "I have no control over this one."

It's common to hear people say something along the lines of "I get into this situation, and I feel afraid, but I don't know why. Then I try to deal with the feeling (fear)." But what they need to deal with is the thought. They need to deal with the belief (or, in this case, limiting belief). When we identify and change a limiting belief, we avoid the negative emotions, and we position ourselves to achieve a desired outcome. The remainder of this book explores several ways to achieve this. Most evolved thinkers believe that conquering yourself is the pathway to changing the world or at least being happy. So why do we resist change?

The author Torben Rick gives us 12 typical reasons for why we resist change.[2] They are as follows:

1. Misunderstanding about the reason for a change
2. Fear of the unknown
3. Lack of competence
4. Connected to the old way
5. Low trust
6. Temporary fad
7. Not being consulted or a part of the process of change
8. Poor communication
9. Changes to routines
10. Exhaustion / Saturation
11. Change in the status quo
12. Benefits and rewards

These are other examples of limiting beliefs that create a resistance to change. How do we further break down our resistance to change so that we can overcome it? That involves a willingness to think differently. I will use a contemporary example in business and then explain further.

Despite a recent swirl of bad press from isolated and egregious offense, Uber has become a tremendous success from an entrepreneurial or business model perspective. Uber is a German word that means "above," "over," or "across." Based in San Francisco, Uber has taken the place of the traditional taxicab service with an innovative ride-sharing service that

2. Rick, T. (2011, May 23). Top 12 Reasons Why People Resist Change. Retrieved May 5, 2015, from http://www.torbenrick.eu/blog/change-management/12-reasons-why-people-resist-change/

has changed the landscape of transportation. Uber created a smartphone app that connects their passengers with drivers of vehicles to hire. There's no money transferred from hand to hand. Both drivers and customers are rated, so there are some unique features of safety and comfort in it. (Although recently, these features have failed to protect customers and have yielded significantly bad results in isolated areas.)

In a recent article entitled "Taxis versus Uber: A Perfect Example of Resistance to Change,"[3] we pick up clues on our resistance to change and how we move beyond it.

At the core of the article is the fact that businesses and business leaders remain "prisoners of an old way of thinking and entrenched in the defense of an aging system,"[4] whereas innovative thinkers move past small and restrictive thinking. They overcome the resistance to change that their environment is telling them exists.

As I mentioned previously, the root of the resistance to change is the limiting belief. When we accurately assess the source of resistance in our thinking, we can "rewire" a more desirable set of thoughts, replacing the limiting belief with a preferable and more rewarding

3. Bouqet, C. & Renault, C. (2014, September 6). Taxis vs Uber: A Perfect Example of Resistance to Change. Retrieved May 5, 2015, from http://www.nbr.co.nz/article/taxis-vs-uber-perfect-example-resistance-change

4. Bouqet, C. & Renault, C. (2014, September 6). Taxis vs Uber: A Perfect Example of Resistance to Change. Retrieved May 5, 2015, from http://www.nbr.co.nz/article/taxis-vs-uber-perfect-example-resistance-change

set of beliefs. As a result, you hit your goal or get what you are looking for.

That's what Rewired is all about: reversing those thoughts that hold us captive and imprisoned by static thinking.

Another example of resistance to change comes from international sports. 1954, John Landy said the following:

> Frankly, I think the four-minute mile is beyond my capabilities. Two seconds may not sound much, but to me it's like trying to break through a brick wall. Someone may achieve the four-minute mile the world is wanting so desperately, but I don't think I can.[5]

Imagine the backdrop for this comment. In 1945, the world record time for the mile was 4:01.3. Nine years later, on May 6, 1954, Roger Bannister crashed through the 4-minute barrier in Oxford in 3:59.4. What most people don't know is the story of Rogers rival, John Landy.

Starting in 1952, John ran races consistently in the low 4:02 range. He then famously launched the quote above as a proclamation – "for me, it just can't be done." Then Roger broke the 4-minute barrier, and what happened next? Forty-six days later, John Landy ran a 3:57.9! It was almost unimaginable. Why Johns performance

---

5. Mind vs Matter | The Science of Sport (2009, January 14). Retrieved May 5, 2015, from http://sportsscientists.com/2009/01/mind-vs-matter/

changed so dramatically after Rogers record-breaking effort continues to be hotly debated. But it is also the underpinning of this book; "Whether you think you can, or you think you can't – you are right" (Henry Ford). This business about what we believe as "truth" is both liberating and at times debilitating. Bottom line? We have to find a way past our mental barriers.

The power of great coaching provides a confidential partnership to identify our limitations accurately and rewire our thinking for positive outcomes. Having the right person in your life to help navigate these areas where we are blind often produces unprecedented and accelerated growth personally and professionally.

As another example, perhaps you want to go to the next level of leadership. The company is going to provide the usual transition training to get you up to speed on your new role. At this point, you don't have any limiting belief, at least that you're aware of, that prevents you from getting involved in the transition training. You just lack competence (the third of the previous list of 12 typical reasons we resist change). Your conscious mind is aware and says, "Look, I've never been at this level. I don't have the reference points (yet)." Consequently, you have the typical low-grade performance anxiety in the transition because you are in new territory but still want to feel confident even in transition.

Now it gets trickier. You've finished the transition, are going to meetings, and you are fearful. Then you have to assess what could be happening in the subconscious mind. Is there a limiting belief going on in the background? Does it date back to high school when you got pinned in a wrestling tournament before the home crowd, and your dad gave you the silent treatment on the ride home? As a young woman, was it becoming President of the Student Council and bombing your first important public speech?

What goes on in the subconscious is potent, and for progression to occur, it has to be assessed and overcome.

New Solutions to Old Problems

The good news about *Rewired* is there is hope outside of clinical therapy. It's about overcoming the resistance to change in our thinking. It's about overcoming the limiting beliefs, and it's less about modifying your negative emotions through positive affirmation. An elevated definition of positive affirmation could be to rewire negative thoughts with positive ones. But to be true to "thine own self," you have to know what the limiting beliefs are.

The same holds true when you want to go to the next level of commitment in a significant or intimate relationship. Intellectually, you know what that means. You know a few good books on relationships and marriage, and you believe you will nail it. You even have some favorite websites for compelling and humorous tips on how to do it.

But once you go to the next level of commitment, you become cynical, suspicious or controlling. As hard as you try to put into practice ideas from trusted sources, the negative thoughts and emotions have taken over and rooted. And then you ask yourself like I did 20 years ago, "How can I be so capable in so many areas, and so incompetent in meaningful relationships?" It happens because there is a story in the subconscious mind, and unless you go in *Commando SEAL Team 6* style and root out the enemy, it is not going to change. First you must accept the need to change and identify the negative emotions about the change. Then you need to find someone you can trust to dig deeper and discuss with you the thoughts that are attached to this particular area or personal desire for growth, progress, and success. Great coaching is designed to get to the root of our thoughts without getting tangled in the negative emotions that distract us from the source of our issue.

Much like a runner using a drogue chute, a limiting belief places an artificial resistance on your personal potential and performance. The limiting belief is a belief we hold that's counter-productive to what we want. It is a conviction or a generalization that's accepted as truth, and it keeps us stuck until it is identified, contested, and overturned.

Limiting beliefs keep us from taking risks; they paralyze us. We stop raising our hand in class, going to the podium for the two-minute thank you speech, taking the fast ride at Magic Mountain, and jumping into the right seat of our friend's brand new Corvette. As soon as we stop taking risks, we move backward. Then we become captive to our fears and our small thinking. Risk-taking is a big part of helping people attack the limiting belief and move onto "the next big thing."

A limiting belief keeps us stuck. Not only have we stopped taking risks, but we've stopped taking responsibility as well. Why? It's easier to blame other people than it is to face our own issue. And we wonder why we avoid it.

Once we have identified the limiting beliefs, we can change them. What allows us to do this is a rewiring of the mind, known as neuroplasticity (more on this in Chapter 5). This is the science of personal transformation, and it is the new frontier for great coaching. Helping people move away from archaic systems of thought and toward new and exciting approaches is what *Rewired* is all about.

Chapter takeaway: Ray Davis said, "A challenge only becomes an obstacle when you bow to it." By identifying our limiting belief, we can find the root of our resistance to change. Once we remove undesirable thoughts that we've accepted as "truth," we are on our way to achieving the growth, progress, and success that we desire.

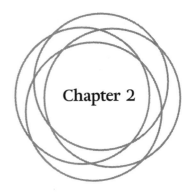

Chapter 2

Why Performance Coaching Can Handle It

"Limits, like fear, are often an illusion."
– Michael Jordan

We begin this chapter with a compelling quote from Michael Jordan that offers us this message: Feeling blocked or getting stuck at times comes from an illusion held in our mind. It is not an actual boundary or a barrier. It is imposed on us, and we need to clarify and uncover it to get over it. Then we can create a more evolved or superior way of thinking and obtain a desired outcome.

The Performance Envelope

I had the privilege of serving our country as a lieutenant in the U.S. Navy. The sense of fulfilling a duty and commitment to our country and playing a pivotal role made me feel as though I was living out an intended purpose. As a designated Naval Aerospace Physiologist, I received an even greater privilege: a chance to go through the primary flight-training program in Pensacola, Florida.

One of the greatest coaching lessons I learned at flight school was from my flight instructor, LCDR Doug Mahilek. Not only did he teach me how to fly a high-performance aircraft (T-34 Charlie), but he also taught me something far more important: how to overcome limiting beliefs in the cockpit. LCDR Mahilek would become one of my greatest mentors in life. I credit him with my success under his instruction. Out of a class of 41 hard charging and ambitious officers, I was one of four to complete the grueling Naval Flight Training Syllabus. And receiving a high-performance rating on my flight certificate opened a few doors as well.

Coaching and the Performance Envelope

Every airplane has what they call a known performance envelope. What that means is this: If it goes below a certain speed, it will stall and fall out of the air. If it goes above a

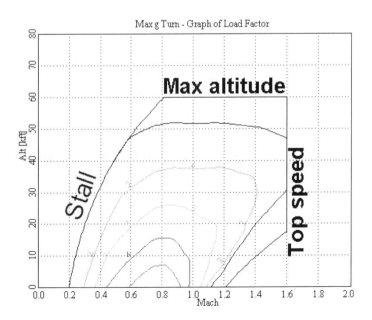

certain speed, the wings will rip off, and it will crash. If it goes above a certain altitude, it will be oxygen-deprived, the motor will be starved, and it will stall. The performance envelope looks like a rectangular box on a graph (similar to below), and it indicates what you can do with the plane.

If you keep the performance of the plane inside the performance envelope, you're going to be safe. If you go outside the envelope, bad things are going to happen.

Unlike airplanes, we can extend our performance envelope so that we can achieve a specific and often superior result in an area. We have all heard about examples of pushing the performance envelope in athletics, like Rodger Bannister's sub-four-minute mile. What is equally impressive is the parallel story of the relatively unknown runner, John Landy, whose story we briefly touched on in the previous chapter.

John Landy's story highlights the fact that our belief about what we are capable of affects our physiological performance. Once Landy's mental barrier was removed – once he was freed from limiting beliefs – he was able to extend his physiological performance envelope.[6]

Once our limiting beliefs are removed, we are capable of achieving our personal best in any category, given that the approach is strategic and intentional.

------

6. Mind vs Matter | The Science of Sport (2009, January 14). Retrieved May 5, 2015, from http://sportsscientists.com/2009/01/mind-vs-matter/

Why Performance Coaching?

The coaching movement has evolved from athletics, into business, and now to the personal realm. What began as life coaching has mutated into specialties that focus on delivering targeted services for targeted outcomes. One of these specialties is performance coaching. Great performance coaches understand the performance envelope and the approach necessary to expand it. Let me explain further.

As I am writing this chapter, I am stuck at the 1:40 lap time at a certain racetrack on my motorcycle. I am going to hire an AMA Pro Racer to get the data, video, and on-track coaching that I need to get me to 1:37. We will look at the following:

1. When I put on the brakes
2. When I open the throttle
3. How close I am to the corner apex
4. What my speed is at any number of points on the track that we determine are necessary

This information will give me numerous opportunities to discover where to make changes. I can break down the challenge into segments with specific goals, work on them individually, and then thread it all back together for a superior outcome.[7]

If you watch football in the U.S. today, you know that there are statistics for everything. If there is a match-up between an offensive wide receiver and a defensive cornerback, the

---

7. On 1/23/2015, at ACS, I broke the barrier and hit my personal best of 1:39.5 with some good coaching from John Hilton.

commentator will quickly tell you each of the men's height, vertical jump, and speed in the 40-yard dash. Why? This data gives coaches and quarterbacks valuable input on key match-up's to exploit weaknesses and capitalize on personal strengths.

Performance coaching does the same thing. In the areas of personal development and achievement, we break down a challenge into elements that can be measured so that we can look for progress. Sometimes it's obvious; other times you have to be creative. Either way, more data points will significantly increase your probability of success. Great coaches know what to measure and, more importantly, how to apply it. It was from this approach that my company, The Performance Group, was born.

When we think of performance today, most people think of a theatrical performance or an athletic performance. However, the original definition of the word "performance" is "the act of carrying into execution an achievement or an accomplishment; to fulfill an intended purpose; to fulfill a duty or a commitment."[8]

When I crafted our company name, I thought about how I wanted to create a company that would help people fulfill their commitments and do what was important to them. I didn't want to help them achieve goals just for the sake of personal ambition. Whether it's losing weight, getting married or making a critical decision, commitment is an

---

8. (n.d.). Retrieved May 5, 2015, from http://www.merriam-webster.com/dictionary/performance

issue. And that's where The Performance Group comes in. We partner with clients to help them fulfill a personal commitment or a milestone event that has value to them. It has even greater meaning to partner with those who have a goal that's attached to their community, company, family, or perhaps a spiritual calling that has intrinsic value.

Performance coaching also has other equally rewarding facets. We provide the motivation, tools, and accountability to guide clients to achieve their bucket list adventure, milestone achievement, or what some might call their personal masterpiece. Whatever your definition of deep, meaningful, or valuable is – we collaborate with you until it is fulfilled.

Performance coaching tends to attract people who are oriented toward statistics, data, or science – the measurable and tangible aspects of the growth process. But it appeals equally to the dreamer who lives and thinks outside the box.

The Performance Group is unique because we integrate the innovative field of neuroscience into the coaching experience with data and experiential learning. Our brains have an innate ability to change physically (neuroplastic) when we are faced with new challenges and experiences. To fully harness the power of this event known as neuroplasticity, you need to challenge your brain with training or experiences that are novel, adaptive, and complete.[9]

---

9. Neuroscience 101: A guide to your amazing brain. (n.d.). Retrieved May 22, 2015, from http://www.lumosity.com/

The secret sauce of performance coaching is the unique packaging of data, experiential learning, and the principles of neuroscience that expands the performance envelope. This innovative approach leads us to shifted paradigms, breakthroughs, and measurable performance growth. This will be discussed in detail in Chapter 5.

Putting Science to the Test

About two years ago, I started racing motorcycles on asphalt at speeds that top out at 175 miles per hour. Before I got involved on that level, I promised my wife that I would get the specialized training necessary to be safe. Other than landing in the emergency room once after a crash to rule out a broken pelvis, it has been the time of my life. Motorcycle racing at my age is a constant reminder: Do not shrink back, quit, or avoid opportunities that have value – even though fear and risk are involved. Mark Twain's words remind me that, "Twenty years from now, we will regret the things we didn't do more than the things we did." The Performance Group helps you identify opportunities that are risky, but valuable – and we partner with you to achieve them.

I'm tickled that I took the risk to ride and race motorcycles later in life. I feel fortunate to be living such a full life at age 51.

Neuroscience, Racing, and Mind Shift

Every once in a while, race organizations will do a fundraiser at the track that will allow you to sit on the backseat of a race bike, with a racing professional, at race speed. This is referred to as the "two-up" ride. Your experience begins by getting outfitted in full race gear. Then you are ushered out to a fully prepped race bike piloted by a professional motorcycle racer. The bike is designed with a handle attached to the gas tank for the person on the back. You climb on the back and hold on to the bar on the tank. It is not for the fainthearted.

My personal experience of the "two-up" was crystallized at Auto Club Speedway in Fontana, California. As we went into Turn 1 at over 120 miles per hour, I thought, "My God, this is really a bad decision." I honestly thought we were going to die.

I had previously jumped out of an airplane and flown an F-18D Hornet Fighter Jet from the rear seat, but this was a whole different animal. As I was completely terrified, something strange happened. After I had realized I was going to live, I saw a new and far greater possibility as a rider and racer. By having this rider take me far out of what I would call my performance envelope, I had a new experiential understanding that extended me into new and superior territory as a rider.

I discovered what it was like to ride at the next level because I had experienced it. It changed my mind – literally. That was a neuroplastic moment for my brain. This is a specific example and practical insight into how our mind can be rewired. Bottom line: You have to experience this to achieve it. This is the proverbial walking over hot coals (which I don't encourage in my practice).

As a result of this experience, I became a faster rider on the racetrack, and I made it to the podium twice while racing at club level, which is a significant accomplishment in Southern California. Thank you, Chris Ulrich, for piloting the bike. I am waiting for the moment when I come out of Turn 3 at Auto Club on a wheelie and direct my bike into Turn 4 by simply leaning in that direction.

Applying the Knowledge of Neuroplasticity

In this book, I have identified three separate areas to evaluate ourselves regarding how happy we are and what our need for personal development is. They are performance (job, hobby, fitness, etc.), relationships, and purpose (spirituality, charity, mentoring, etc.).

Performance coaching that combines science and data with conventional wisdom is innovative and produces lasting results. I believe this is my greatest contribution to coaching. This approach helps people avoid the trap of living for an emotional uplift that provides a temporary solution to a chronic issue.

Mind Shift Versus Positive Psychology

Rewiring your thinking in a particular area is different than positive or motivational thinking. Although the latter strategies can be emotionally rousing, most of their impact is lost unless we have the tools for transformation, which will actually change our thinking.

To get past some of those barriers, we need a mechanism that we can easily identify with and understand. We need structure.

Performance coaching provides that structure and process. For example, someone may have a limiting belief that creates fear of public speaking, undergoing a performance review, or an activity in the sales process. We craft a unique experience with several components to overcome the limiting belief and produce a desired outcome. Here's how:

1. Identify the process, beliefs, and limiting beliefs
2. Identify favorable content and data that will produce a better outcome
3. Identify activities and opportunities within the task to measure progress and isolate sticking points
4. Create a parallel or ideal experience that will create the desired learning effect and outcome

Performance coaching moves us past the limiting belief, "the illusion" that Michael Jordan talked about. This imaginary boundary can be dismantled. In the upcoming chapters, I will cover some revolutionary research about how we can rewire our thoughts.

Some questions to ponder:

1. What do you feel you have passed up or haven't allowed yourself to pursue?

2. If you were able to rewire your thinking, what specifically would you want to develop or master?

Chapter takeaway: Science has given us a valuable peek into the mechanism of change. Performance coaching uses this innovative discovery of rewiring the mind known as neuroplasticity. Far beyond an emotional experience, we use science and data to create real changes and make them stick.

Notes: "Follow your heart," is a popular piece of advice in the secular world. I think it's connected to purpose and what we were designed to do (discussed in detail later in the book). The challenge, however, is that our rational (conscious) mind wants to keep us safe, and it creates safe thoughts that become barriers to fulfilling our deeper dreams and ambitions.

Part 1

Performance

Chapter 3

Power Meter:

Risk, Value, and Need

The first part of this book deals with relationships. Now we will shift into the realm of performance.

Twenty years from now you will be more disappointed by the things that you didn't do than by the things you did. So throw off the bowlines. Sail away from the safe harbor. Catch the trade winds in your sails. Explore. Dream. Discover.

– Mark Twain

We are hard-wired for adventure – we are dreamers. However, as we get older, it becomes more difficult to take risks. Unfulfilled opportunities, broken promises, or even worse – deep wounds inflicted by our own decisions or someone else's – hinder us. The days race by, and we cuddle up to our favorite routines rather than take the right risks. What is the result? We become bored, cynical, or filled with regret.

Risk + Value

How can we throw off the bowlines, leave the safe harbor, and catch the next available wind when it's risky business? It depends on how you define risk and what is motivating it. In his book, *Failing Forward*, John Maxwell tells us "Risk should not be assessed on the success of the outcome, or the fear it produces, but on the value it brings."[10]

When my clients talk about something completely out of the box, like summiting Everest or spearing a large fish in a single breath hold, we go down a rabbit hole; where is the value in it? Most risks involve fear and reward, but without value in the equation, your risk might not be worth the price of admission.

Here are some examples of values when you are considering risk[11]:

1. Power (authority, control)
2. Precision (work in situations where there is little tolerance for error)
3. Challenge (stimulates full use of your potential)
4. Change and variety (varied, frequently changing work responsibilities and work settings)
5. Competition (your abilities against others where there is a clear win or lose outcome)

---

10. Maxwell, J. (2000). *Failing Forward*. Nashville, Tennessee: Thomas Nelson.

11. Vanourek, B. & Vanourek, G. (n.d.). Triple Crown Leadership. Retrieved May 5, 2015, from http://triplecrownleadership.com/resources/personalvaluesexercise/

We have to consider the value before we take the necessary risk to achieve our goal.

Risk + Need

We can further clarify the value of a risk by assessing how our risks are meeting a need. Many people miss the mark on how basic need drives our desires. There is a newfound reward in risk taking when we connect it to fulfilling a need. It provides context and deeper meaning to the achievement. One of the tools we use to connect need and risk taking is the "Essential Six." This tool is a modified version from the Madanes and Robbins' six human needs[12], which is a tool they adopted from Maslow's hierarchy of needs.

These needs are:
1.   **Belonging** – being in meaningful relationships
2.   **Growth** – seeing growth in targeted areas
3.   **Certainty** – a need for structure, routine
4.   **Uncertainty** – the need for mystery, adventure, romance
5.   **Contribution** – to bring benefit to others
6.   **Significance** – to fulfill a calling, a mission, or a purpose

We help our clients to assess risks by clarifying the value it brings, and we help them to understand the need it is ful-

12. Madanes, C. (n.d.) Six Human Needs Test "Robbins Madanes Coach Training." Retrieved May 5, 2015, from http://robbinsmadanescoachtraining.com/six-human-needs-test/

filling. When we talk about risk and value, and we connect them with our basic needs, what is driving us becomes very clear. After making that clear, we either modify the idea or boldly push forward with the plan.

When significant risk appears to be tied to money, ego, or something purely selfish, it needs to pass what I call the litmus test of a peer review to move forward safely. Say I want to ride my bicycle from Los Angeles to New York or break the 200-mile per hour mark at the Bonneville Salt Flats. Then I must first present the idea to my wife and kids. *After* I have done that, I share my idea with a jury of peers that have different backgrounds to flesh out the motivation. (The LA-NY ride is for charity. The 200-mile per hour barrier? Well, the jury is out on that one.)

Bottom line? There are different ways to fulfill a need, and at times, a creative and less risky approach can meet that need.

Right Risk = Value + Need

Mark Twain opened my eyes to my Mission, which is to coach people to take the right risks so that they will live fulfilled lives. Even if they fail, they can look in the rearview mirror and say, "You know what? That opportunity came, and I didn't shrink from it."

Here is an example of how the elements of risk, value, and need all come together. In 2006, a friend invited me to crew his J-120 sailboat from New York to the Bahamas. It would be just three of us in the well-built 40-foot boat covering 1,127-nautical miles of the Atlantic. My motive? At the time, I was a minister and cared very deeply about my friend who invited me. What was motivating me to take this risk? I knew I would have five full days to talk to him about his faith and his family. For me, it was fulfilling the need for significance – this was my mission in life.

I remember thinking, "How hard can it be to sail a boat?" I grew up fishing with my dad in open ocean waters, and I had surfed all around the world and in big surf. However, I didn't have much sailing experience.

We, the crew, met briefly the night before we set out to discuss the overarching plan. We had a weather report on the table that was calling for 10 to 14-foot seas north of Cape Hatteras, directly on our travel route. Being a surfer, I knew what this meant and told the other two sailors that the weather report "concerned me."

The skipper replied, "It's fine. We'll be safe. Those are open water swells (swells that don't break)." Then he said, "Plus the J-120 is designed to roll completely to its upright position due to the weight of the keel." I thought, "Wow, what a relief." If we happened to "roll" the boat at night in 50-degree water, at least if it capsized, the boat would right itself. I thought, "That sounds like a pretty rock-solid plan. I'm in."
Two nights later, at midnight, about 250 nautical miles into the trip, 10 to 14-foot seas were crashing in the cockpit. At that time, I was comforted by this thought: "Well, my wife

could remarry someone with a better risk management profile." Tethered into the cockpit by a four-point restraint harness, we took turns doing battle in 45 miles per hour winds until we had an electrical failure. The last recorded maximum speed was 28 knots. That's fast for a sailboat.

Far outside of my comfort zone, I was frightened. Not to mention the fear I felt from watching all those National Geographic shows about rogue waves and waiting for that five-story wall of water to come and swallow us whole. Mark Twain also wrote, "Courage is not the absence of fear, but the mastery of it." Well, I was far from mastering it. As I went below deck that night, I felt completely rattled and defeated. We stayed in those conditions for another 100 nautical miles that night. We had to cut the trip short because of wind damage, so we "put in" in North Carolina at Cape Fear, which was both funny and ironic. Although we were unable to reach the Bahamas, I stretched far out of my comfort zone for a valuable reason. Not to mention that we had an incredible experience together and a great story to tell.

Final assessment? There was value beyond the element of adventure or friendship. This was the right risk.

Risk = Value + Need

"Only those who will risk going too far can possibly find out how far we can go." That's an interesting quote from T.S. Eliot. I'm not going to be a proponent of telling people to go "too far." However, performance coaching is about helping you go a lot further than you thought that you could go. It's about extending the personal limitations of your belief system and your abilities to glean new and rewarding experiences. You feel alive because your basic needs are being met. You are growing in areas that are relevant and rewarding. If you are lucky, you can contribute to others and discover significance in this season of your life, which too few have found a way to do.

To me, Mark Twain's quote has become a call to help people avoid the crippling effects of regret. The solution is to understand your need, clarify the value in the goal, and come up with a plan. Then we jump together. Lao Tzu said, "When I let go of what I am, I become what I might be."

Chapter takeaway: The power in performance is restored when we determine the right risk, define the value, and identify our personal need. *Rewired* is about letting our goals be driven by value rather than ego. That's when we move the needle on the power meter. Together, let's rewire the risk. Let's explore, dream, and discover.

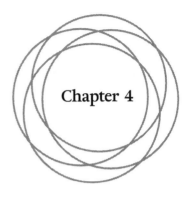

Power Lines:

Aligning Values and Beliefs with Intrinsic Motive

> *"The purposes of a man's heart are deep waters,*
> *but a man of understanding draws them out."*
> — Proverbs 20:5

Deep Waters

Some define deep waters as revealing the deep secrets of their past. For others, it's just the opposite; it's about the dream of doing what they've always wanted to but were afraid of. For all of us, it means being vulnerable – and it's scary to put ourselves out there.

The writer of the Proverb above connects deep water with the concept of our "purpose." I agree with him. We all feel as though we were created for a particular purpose. Call it your sweet spot; call it your passion. But most agree that when you are doing what you believe you were purposed to do, it's powerful. You lose track of time, you forget to eat and take care of other necessities because you are fueled by something that's internal or intrinsic.

For our clients, the end game typically points toward finding their intrinsic value. The coaching process is not about telling them what their intrinsic values are. It's rather about drawing out these values through a series of questions, tools, and experiences. It's about removing the clutter and impurities to help them to discover the answers themselves. For a coach, listening and waiting are very powerful tools. This chapter is about moving from the shallow end of the pool (what is safe, predictable, or pleasing to others) to the "deep waters." It's about moving from lower level motive (conscious mind) to higher ground (values, beliefs, intrinsic motive) of the subconscious mind. It's about finding the guts to pursue the dream goal, dream career, or dream partner. In other words, it's about living the dream. It's about aligning our values and beliefs to unlock the subconscious mind, because science has told us that this is where your imagination, intuition, and dreams live.

The iceberg diagram depicted in Chapter 1 tells us that the conscious mind guides the logistics of life. But the subconscious mind is where we find the "deep waters" that the writer of Proverbs 20:5 spoke of. In our subconscious, we risk doing what we've always wanted to do but are often afraid to do – what our imagination and intuition tell us are possible. The conscious mind wants us to be safe; the subconscious wants us to be deeply fulfilled and satisfy what some would term "a calling," others "a destiny."

* Short term memory is the ready state of the conscious mind.[13]

Beliefs

In the coaching relationship, we gain a better understanding of our beliefs held in the subconscious mind through the tools and assessment phase. All of us frame our world view from our belief system. Here is a partial list of common belief systems we discuss:

- Religion
- Science
- Philosophy
- Morality
- Atheism
- New Age / Spiritualism

It is always rewarding to watch clients untangle conflicting beliefs once we clearly define their values and discuss tangible ways of living them out.

In our coaching practice, the diagram below[14] is a springboard to understanding what drives certain choices and behaviors. It's an excellent exercise that brings great clarity.

---

13. Wilson, E.O. (1999). Consilience: The Unity of Knowledge. New York, New York: Random House.

14. Attitudes, Beliefs and Values. (n.d.). Retrieved May 5, 2015, from http://docmo. hubpages.com/hub/Teaching-and-Assessing-Attitudes

Values

Our beliefs are deeply held assumptions about life, which stem from religion, experiences, and other sources. From these beliefs, we form our values. Our attitudes and actions are driven by our beliefs and values.

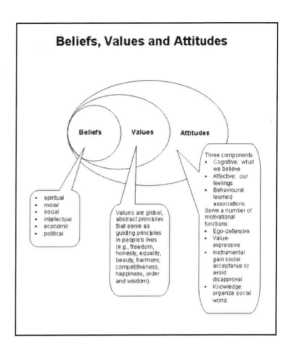

I've met many people who confess feeling lost, confused, or insecure – even though most of their life is dialed in and organized. Some look for a root cause connected to a troubling event of the past. Others have avoided the psychoanalysis simply by defining their values clearly. It is priceless to watch relief sweep over someone's face when they realize that they are not damaged or victimized, just unclear about their beliefs and values.

One of my favorite quotes is from Albert Einstein: "If you can't explain it simply, you just don't understand it well enough." That's the magic in great coaching; profound is sometimes simple; it's just not easy.

Here is an additional list of values[15]:

- Loyalty (steadfastness and allegiance)
- Pleasure (enjoyment)
- Power (authority, control)
- Precision (work in situations where there is little tolerance for error)
- Responsibility (being accountable for results)
- Recognition (getting acknowledged for your contribution)
- Stability (work routine and have largely predictable duties)
- Spirituality

Although the events that took place in 1994 were humbling, the transformation etched a new set of beliefs in stone for me. A set of values followed my newly adopted beliefs. These values are also built into our company.

These six values are:

1. Spirituality
2. Wisdom
3. Family
4. Achievement
5. Innovation
6. Adventure

Find your values and have the courage to build a life around them.

---

15. Vanourek, B. & Vanourek, G. (n.d.). Triple Crown Leadership. Retrieved May 5, 2015, from http://triplecrownleadership.com/resources/personalvaluesexercise/

Intrinsic Motivation

A thorough examination of motives is outside the scope this book, but let's define extrinsic and intrinsic motivation.

Extrinsic motivation is also known as the stick and carrot, reward and punishment motivation. It is the reward we get from an achievement such as a large salary, bigger house, faster car, better clothing, more jewelry, prestige, etc. Extrinsic motivation can also involve the opportunity to compete with and beat another person.

In a corporate sense, extrinsic motivation is often referred to as the "pay for performance plan." It means that you are hired to do a job and perform, and that's the bottom line. Employers are less concerned about your motives and more concerned about results.

One the other hand,

Intrinsic motivation refers to behavior that is driven by internal rewards. Intrinsic motivation occurs when we act without any obvious external rewards. We simply enjoy an activity or see it as an opportunity to explore, learn, and actualize our potentials.[16]

---

16. Cherry, K. (n.d.). What is Intrinsic Motivation? Retrieved May 5, 2015, from http://psychology.about.com/od/motivation/f/intrinsic-motivation.htm

Dan Pink, the author of *Drive: The Surprising Truth About What Motivates Us*, says,

Science has now confirmed what we know in our hearts: the secret to achieving high performance isn't rewards and punishments but it's the unseen, intrinsic drive, the drive to do things for their own sake. [17]

Dan Pink has authored five bestselling books on leadership, business, and motivation. His summary finding for us on this topic is "traditional rewards aren't always as effective as we think."

In a TEDtalk in July of 2009 in Oxford, England, Dan masterfully explains, "there is a mismatch between what science knows and what business does."[18] Using a "robust" body of research, Dan untangles the prevailing belief that better performance at work comes from a "rewards based incentive approach."

In problems that have a simple set of rules, and a clear destination – the rewards based [extrinsic] motivation model works. But in the 21st century where we are called to innovate and create, the research does not support this model.[19]

---

17. Pink, D. (1995). *Drive: The Surprising Truth about What Motivates Us*. New York, New York: Penguin Group.

18. Transcript of "The puzzle of motivation" (n.d.). Retrieved May 5, 2015, from http://www.ted.com/talks/dan_pink_on_motivation/transcript?language=en

19. Transcript of "The puzzle of motivation" (n.d.). Retrieved May 5, 2015, from http://www.ted.com/talks/dan_pink_on_motivation/transcript?language=en

The jury is in: We need to understand and integrate intrinsic motive better to achieve greater results.

Bringing in Alignment

In 2011, I crashed my motorcycle on the racetrack. I spent the day in the ER to rule out a broken pelvis. The following six weeks, I used chiropractic, electrical nerve stimulation (TENS), physical therapy, and massage therapy to heal and regain my strength. I was amazed at how quickly I recovered by aligning those four modalities. It was a testimony to aligning the right ingredients to maximize a favorable outcome. The same holds true for personal growth opportunities: Aligning values, beliefs, and intrinsic motive is key to aligning the power that sustains elevated performance.

Case Study:

One of our recent clients shared about the power of aligning these elements in our coaching immersion:

I was at a crossroad that involved either cementing a future in something I was not passionate about or starting from a fresh perspective. I had to make a seemingly impossible choice of giving up the practice of Law. I wrestled with this choice for three days with Joel at his 72-hour Immersive Coaching Experience. We assessed my reality, confronted my fears, and experienced an "aha" moment when we clarified my values and identified what internally [intrinsically] motivated me. Through a diverse approach that pulled from neuroscience, philosophy, theology, psychology, data, and research, we quickly began to integrate the best parts of me, my unique abilities, and my advanced skill set from Law. We cast a compelling new vision that challenges my intellect and positions me to form strategic alliances, build global coherence, and celebrate risk taking for the sake of innovation. Our coaching engagement provided the confidence to pursue a new direction that being a traditional lawyer would never satisfy.

It was a simple approach for our client. He needed to move from his conscious mind (doing what seems logical) to his subconscious mind (doing what inspires him).

Aligning Intrinsic Motive

Here is how we do it:

1. Differentiate conscious and subconscious thought
2. Discuss limiting beliefs about goal or outcome
3. Define your beliefs, values, and attitudes about the goal
4. Identify intrinsic and extrinsic motive or rewards
5. Align intrinsic motive, belief, and values with specific goal
6. Set up an action plan with measurable sub-goals
7. Accountability

Chapter takeaway: When our values and beliefs are aligned with an intrinsic motivation, we're capable of spectacular results. It is about aligning the right opportunity with the right motive to achieve the best result. As Dan Pink reminds us,

[I]f we repair the mismatch between science and business, if we bring our motivation, notions of motivation into the 21st century, if we get past this lazy, dangerous, ideology of carrots and sticks, we can strengthen our businesses, we can solve a lot of [...] [our business] problems, and maybe, maybe —we can change the world.[20]

---

20. Transcript of "The puzzle of motivation" (n.d.). Retrieved May 5, 2015, from http://www.ted.com/talks/dan_pink_on_motivation/transcript?language=en

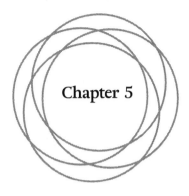

Chapter 5

High-Speed Connection:

Experiential Learning, Data Acquisition, and Neuroscience

> *"An invasion of armies can be resisted,*
> *but not an idea whose time has come."*
>
> – Victor Hugo

High-Speed Connection

Everyone wants things fast, and opportunities for personal growth are no exception. The purpose of this chapter is to show how to create an accelerated growth experience. We do it by combining the right elements of training and content in an immersive learning experience to expose our mind to as much targeted sensory input as possible. By doing so, we rewire new circuits of the mind for favorable results. We believe this is our unique service offering at The Performance Group.

Rewire Your Mind

The underlying premise of this book, *Rewired*, is to remind us that the brain is capable of changing unwanted patterns of thought that have produced undesirable outcomes like anxiety, cynicism, and hopelessness to name a few. In her book *Neuroscience for Leadership*, Tara Swart discusses three simple elements required to create new connections between neurons that can help us move past limiting beliefs. These are focused attention, deliberate repetition, and the right environment.

Focused Attention

If you want to keep your brain agile, you're going to have to hone in on parts of the brain that you use less frequently, says Swart. And this new task has to be so challenging that you'll feel mentally and physically exhausted after practicing the task because you're forcing your brain to work in ways it is unaccustomed to. This is the only way you'll actually grow new neurons strong enough to connect with existing neurons, forming new pathways.

For those who want to stimulate their brain, Swart recommends learning a new language or musical instrument. Or any "energy intensive" challenge that requires 'conscious processing of inputs, conscious decision making, complex problem solving, memorizing complex concepts, planning, strategizing, self-reflection, regulating our emotions and channeling energy from them, exercising self-control and willpower,' Swart says.

Deliberate Repetition and Practice

You can't just learn a new language or musical instrument and never think about it again; you'll forget what you learned. New connections and pathways are fragile, says Swart, and only through repetition and practice can those connections be established enough to become habitual or default behaviors.

She writes in *Neuroscience*: 'Depending on the complexity of the activity, [experiments have required] four and a half months, 144 days or even three months for a new brain map, equal in complexity to an old one, to be created in the motor cortex.'

During this time, motivation, willpower, and self-control are necessary to achieve your goal.

The Right Environment

Without the right environment to enable change, your brain won't be able to focus on what's needed to create new neurons. Instead, your brain will be stuck in survival mode, meaning it will choose to travel along pathways it's already familiar with to mitigate risk

'[The brain's] need [to survive] focuses attention on the sources of danger and on trying to predict where the next threat will appear, on escape or full frontal battle rather than on an innovative or creative solution, on avoiding risk rather than managing it towards a new suite of products, market or way of doing business,' Swart writes. 'And of course, the most important part of our environment is other people and our relationship with them.'

To have the energy to keep your brain flexible and 'plastic,' Ancona and Swart say your physical health needs to be in good shape, especially since your brain sucks up such a massive amount of your body's nutrients. The hydration, nutrients, and rest you need are even more important as your brain learns, unlearns, and relearns behavioral patterns.

'Your brain will send its resources through the blood supply to areas that it can tell that you're focusing attention and concentration on,' Swart tells Fast Company, 'or areas that you have a desire to put more energy into.'[21]

At The Performance Group, we uniquely combine experiential learning, the principles of neuroscience, and data to create an environment that allows for accelerated learning. Because the mind can be rewired when it is exposed to new experiences, we use dynamic learning environments such as racetracks, jump platforms, and combats scenarios to accelerate learning and development. We also use sensory deprivation (float) tanks to focus the mind on targeted change.

---

21. Giang, V. (2015, April 28). What it Takes To Change Your Brain's Patterns After Age 25. Retrieved May 5, 2015, from http://www.fastcompany.com/3045424/work-smart/what-it-takes-to-change-your-brains-patterns-after-age-25

Experiential Learning

Experiential or immersive learning is a potent tool to accelerate learning. As a Naval Officer, we put aviators and aircrew members through two days of high-risk activities that simulated potential threats to achieving their mission. Step one was in the classroom. It was necessary but comparatively boring. Then we got our students into a simulated helicopter device that was dropped into 75-degree pool water, rotated upside down, and submerged 10 feet. Takeaway? Students engaged with greater enthusiasm through experiential learning compared to classroom instruction. This is why we incorporate experiential learning in our coaching approach. This is well supported in the research:

By engaging students in learning activities, immersion may make important concepts and relationships more salient and memorable, helping learners to build more accurate mental models.[22]

Data Acquisition

As an exercise physiologist in a cardiac rehabilitation unit, we monitored the patients' exercise and measured everything from changes in their ECG, heart rate, and blood pressure to rating perceived exertion (RPE). The result? The more feedback we were able to give our patients from their measured data, the more motivated and secure they were about their

---

22. (n.d.). Retrieved May 5, 2015, from http://www.socialinformation.org/readings/ MMORPG%20learning/Dede%201999.pdf

progress. Lesson learned? If you are going to invest the time, money, and effort into coaching, then you need to make sure you measure the right things. What we measure is what we will improve.

Our coaching practice provides tangible ways to measure where we are and where we want to go. We measure what matters. We focus our energy on activities that directly influence achieving the goal. For example, we can use data (reaction time, communication, and leadership skills) measured in a simulated combat scenario that can be directly applied to job performance. It can be dynamic (riding a motorcycle, racing a car, firing a gun at a target), or static (cognitive, emotional, physiological). Either way, we look at a myriad of ways to gather and acquire data, reports, graphs, or charts to bring the targeted result. We craft experiences that give us relevant data, which in turn improves our sense of progress, as well as performance.

Applying the Principles of Neuroscience

Neuroscience is becoming a new frontier in coaching. It allows us to understand how the mind changes when faced with novel experiences. If you are stuck, have a phobia, or have a bad experience, the new research is telling us that we no longer need a compensatory strategy to go around the problem. Instead, it can be rewired – a process known as neuroplasticity. This opens the door to an alternative approach to traditional therapy. This is why we combine new activities with great data and content to create a transformative outcome for our clients.

This practical approach is also being used to help our military personnel returning from combat with Post Traumatic Stress Disorder (PTSD). In her book entitled *Switch on Your Brain*[23], Dr. Caroline Leaf explains what happens in the mind of someone who has PTSD:

A person experiences a crushing mental event that alters the structure of the brain. As the person relives the memory of the event, the unwanted [negative] circuit is strengthened, making it worse and more debilitating. By intentionally reframing these memories and creating new positive thoughts, the circuits responsible for this dysfunction are weakened. Once weakened, the neurons will not receive enough signal input, the network will weaken and lose its ability to produce the negative emotions attached to the traumatic event.[24]

Here, neuroplasticity is seen in both directions, both negatively (trauma) and positively (rewiring). It is an exciting new frontier for learning, relearning, and coaching.

---

23. Leaf, C. (2013). *Switch On Your Brain: The Key to Peak Happiness, Thinking, and Health*. Grand Rapids, Michigan: Baker Books.

24. Leaf, C. (2013). *Switch On Your Brain: The Key to Peak Happiness, Thinking, and Health*. Grand Rapids, Michigan: Baker Books.

A New Frontier

In 2013, President Obama created a program called "White House BRAIN." BRAIN is an acronym for Brain Research through Advancing Innovative Neurotechnologies. The (BRAIN) Initiative is part of a new presidential focus aimed at revolutionizing our understanding of the human brain. By accelerating the development and application of innovative technologies, researchers will be able to produce a revolutionary new dynamic picture of the brain that, for the first time, shows how individual cells and complex neural circuits interact in both time and space. Long desired by researchers seeking new ways to treat, cure, and even prevent brain disorders, this picture will fill major gaps in our current knowledge and provide unprecedented opportunities for exploring exactly how the brain enables the human body to record, process, utilize, store, and retrieve vast quantities of information, all at the speed of thought.[25]

A Case Study That Combines Experiential Learning, Data, and Neuroscience

I took a client to the racetrack to drive an F1 prototype race car fully outfitted with data acquisition. When my client came back from driving his laps, we sat down at a computer terminal and got immediate feedback about what he was doing in the race car. We saw his top speed, his speed in

---

25. What is the BRAIN Initiative? (n.d.). Retrieved May 5, 2015, from http://braininitiative.nih.gov/

each corner, when he applied the throttle, what percentage he applied the throttle, when he put the brakes on and how much brake pressure he applied.

As our client returned to discuss the data, he was struggling with his performance and losing motivation to continue driving. Using the data, we quickly isolated a huge weakness: He was under braking the car. Because we could isolate this one area from the data, we were able to correct his driving performance quickly. Result? He shaved 14 seconds off of his lap time and went from dead last (group of 12) to top 3. This was a huge a turnaround for him, and he was ecstatic. More importantly, we transferred the results of his experience into his professional and personal life. He shifted his thinking from competitive to collaborative and resolved conflict in primary relationships.

We bring the same approach to all of our clients. We help clients practically apply lessons learned from their experiences into their job performance and even their personal lives. It's a game changer.

How We Can Apply the Results

In the coaching experience in the example above, we identified performance issues happening in the car (fast/slow, timid/reckless, distracted/ focused, coachable/independent). Then we looked at how these issues played out in the client's personal and professional life. If you are timid in the car, you are probably timid in the office. If you are disinterested in the data from the car, you may be disinterested in the data at work that can help you. If you shut down or get angry when corrected, you may have a hard time letting others assess your leadership style or your presence. It also holds true regarding how you respond to delicate issues in your personal life. Looking at the data and the attitude about the data gives us some great clues on how to enhance performance on a personal or professional level.

Chapter takeaway: If you are stuck, have a fear, or had a bad experience that has capped your performance, don't get drained compensating for it — because it can be *Rewired*. By combining experiential learning, data, and the principles of neuroscience, we help you traverse the learning curve, rewiring your thinking, and get you to your goal effectively.

Part 2
Relationships

Chapter 6

Power Button:

The Paradox of Vulnerability

> *"Vulnerability is the birthplace for connection and the pathway to the feeling of worthiness."*
>
> – Brene Brown

A paradox is something that's counter-intuitive, something that would appear to be completely the opposite. It often engages and interests us because it creates a conflict or seems contradictory. For example, if we feel defeated or discouraged, someone might encourage us to go out and help someone else. In that situation, a lot of people would think, "How can I help somebody else when I can't help myself?" That's a great example of a paradox.

Vulnerability is a paradox and a scary thing, especially for men. You might as well ask a guy to fight nude and not be worried about his genitalia. I know; you didn't need that visual image. Most of us were raised to believe that vulnerability was an opportunity for others to take advantage of us, so the safest play was to show our strong side only.

However, we are hardwired for relationships. When we hide the places we know are flawed, it leads us to feeling disconnected. In business, feeling disconnected leads to getting stuck, feeling isolated, and underperforming. We tend to feel ashamed and fear that people may sense this, so we stay in hiding.

What is the solution? Well, it's a paradox. The answer is a deep and courageous vulnerability. Most of us have to rewire the way we see this before we buy it.

From spending almost two decades in what I call the "trenches of humanity" as a marriage and family minister, I experienced the power of vulnerability. Much like the first time I looked at the rings of Saturn through a high-powered telescope, I just marveled at its power. It was the big warm fuzzy I had missed growing up.

The thought of exposing my fears, needs, and dreams was originally about as appealing to me as that metal pick they use at the dentist to clean between the teeth. When I became a Christian, I finally felt like I could be open about my weaknesses, flaws, and what I was ashamed of. I felt safe for the first time, and the conversation was set up to foster risk taking. I learned some deep things about myself. For instance, I saw that my self-worth was tied directly to achievement.

I experienced the power of learning to forgive myself. I also saw the power of others showing compassion and care, instead of judgment. I witnessed the power of wisdom to heal delicate and broken places. It all took place in what I call a confidential partnership. In this gathering of three or four men, the mysteries and the secrets of the soul were laid bare. It was magical to be in this sacred place. What an amazing experience to see that beyond the fear, shame, and guilt was a path of reward and freedom. I saw the fruit of humility and the power of letting go of self-pity and perfectionism.

In my transition from unspiritual to spiritual, I saw the power of authenticity and vulnerability like never before. It had an immediate impact on my marriage. My marriage had been filled with bitterness, deceit, and hopelessness. Now it was not only rebuilt, but it also became a fountain of life and a source of joy.

My thinking was rewired. Vulnerability and authenticity were the gateways to this resurrected marriage. It was a new beginning and way of thinking about all relationships. I began to experience a paradox: There was strength in revealing my feelings, uncertainties, and even weaknesses to others. This was unimaginable. This shift in mindset was confirmed when I stood at a major crossroad in my marriage. I was faced with a defining moment: Do I tell my wife the truth about my inner thought life, the secret side that most everyone lives with? Or do I live with a safer watered down version? I put on the parachute and jumped. I thought this could play out in one of three ways. I would: 1) die on impact, 2) be eaten by sharks, or 3) experience what poets and philosophers had told me, but I wasn't buying – that this type of living and loving gives sight to the blind.

Outcome number 3 prevailed. For the first time, as the quote by Brene Brown attests, I experienced a connection and sense of belonging that heightened my sense of value and worthiness. It was a metamorphosis, also known as Meta-noia – a transformational shift in thought from a spiritual experience.[26]

This experience compelled me to help others create this circle of trust, where people could reveal themselves without judgment and receive great feedback to overcome the myth that vulnerability will destroy us.

It has become a centerpiece for working with companies at their top tier of leadership. And the jury is in: If the leadership team is transparent and knows how to build trust, businesses soar because employees feel safe to take risks, collaborate and innovate. Appropriate vulnerability is the key to success in this area. At The Performance Group, we accomplish this specifically for companies by:

1. Clarifying definitions of roles and terminologies related to culture and performance
2. Identifying and removing limiting beliefs from our history that prevent vulnerability

26. Anton, E.J. (2005). *Repentance*. Waltham, Massachusetts: D.P.I.

3. Creating an ideal process and dialogue for real work scenarios that create targeted outcomes

The Power Button

Vulnerability is an internally available power that pays immediate dividends and will transform you, your company, and your relationships. It takes being willing to be seen at our deepest levels, but it yields great returns. It will open the door to opportunities because it takes courage to be vulnerable. Vulnerability helps us become authentic, and it lets us discover that we are enough in our core being.

But there is a caveat: To the untrained eye, what seems like vulnerability could also be a flimsy veil for self-pity, perfectionism, or a judgmental attitude, which is self-centered, attacking and destructive. When leadership doesn't create a culture that taps into the power of vulnerability, people gripe, teams tank, and the culture stagnates.

A Coach's Coach

Jimmy Valvano was a basketball coach at North Carolina State University. He led his team to win the NCAA Basketball Tournament against "long odds."[27] In 1993, he gave his "Don't Ever Give Up" speech at the ESPY Awards (hosted by ESPN). In his speech, there was an element of vulnerability that was electrifying. He talked about his connection to his father

---

27. Jim Valvano. (n.d.). Retrieved May 5, 2015, from http://en.wikipedia.org/wiki/Jim_Valvano

and their belief in each other. He was wholehearted and uncompromising about his ideals and his vision for himself and others, yet he was very comfortable talking about his flaws and his weaknesses. I believe this draws people to each other when it's done appropriately. It is the Power Button — the paradox of putting ourselves out in front of others fully to be seen while hanging on to the best parts of us.

Brene Brown, the well-known researcher, psychologist, and speaker said,

The difficult thing is that vulnerability is the first thing I look for in you and the last thing I'm willing to show you [in me]. In you, it's courage and daring. In me, it's weakness risking exposure of self and weakness to have a relationship.[28]

Brene hits the nail on the head: We all want it, but we are deathly afraid of it. The paradox of going to this scary place is that it also opens the door to joy, creativity, and acceptance, which helps us feel loved and connected. Great companies cultivate professional relationships that are genuine and have appropriate levels of affection and trust.

Anyone can put their finger on this powerful tool and watch its power unfold. What is the result? People begin to show up and serve as a gateway and birthplace for creativity. And being in healthy relationships blows the door open to proper risk-taking and growth.

---

28. The Power of Vulnerability. (n.d.). Retrieved May 5, 2015, from https://www.ted. com/talks/brene_brown_on_vulnerability?language=en

What is the paradox? The lunacy of such openness becomes "the secret sauce" that builds and sustains these rewarding relationships. And it redefines cultural terms like courage and helps people overcome the fear of being rejected and chronically underperforming.

Pushing the power button of vulnerability engages the courageous self. It keeps the door to our personal strengths open while also opening the door to our weaknesses and struggles. And when we integrate our "whole story," we become more fully known to other people, which is highly rewarding and fulfilling.

When our goals are consistently blocked, and we feel disconnected from people and isolated from sources that can help us, it is nearly impossible to navigate a solution successfully. Until we do, we will stay unfulfilled and disconnected in relationships.

Some studies suggest that it is more destructive for children to be abandoned than it is for them to be beaten. The reason is that even in relationships where children are beaten, they have a connection with others, whereas when they are abandoned, they have no connection.

When we push the power button of vulnerability, we become wholehearted. Our hearts begin to fill up because we're no longer afraid of being completely known. Secondly, we get a new sense of courage from being comfortable in our own skin, warts and all. Thirdly, we begin to let go of who we should be for who we are.

When we begin to experience the power of vulnerability, we leave behind our mask. We become the first to tell other people that we love them. We are strong enough to love people who might not be in a position to love us back. At work, we are strong enough to find solutions for someone who is responding poorly to us.

Plotting the Success of Vulnerability
Here are several ways we can create an atmosphere of vulnerability:

1. When appropriate, lead the conversation or meeting with balancing your strengths, weaknesses, needs, and hopes.
2. Be careful to praise others with specific and accurate comments.
3. Always present criticism in a context of optimism and a commitment to assisting their growth.
4. Define and verbalize your professional commitment to them
5. Remind them of the goal in terms that are consistent with the company's culture and mission statement. For example, "We are all about loyalty, not perfection."

We have to win the battle of vulnerability. If we don't, we will become numb, withdraw, and go into hiding. In business, we will isolate ourselves, become fearful, and stop taking risks. On top of all this, we become unhappy people. As Brene Brown reminds us, "numbing out in one area will cause us to also numb out in other areas that we want to feel alive in."[29]

Vulnerability is a simple strategy that allows us to be seen at deeper levels. It opens the door to better relationships, greater performances, a more rewarding life, and living out our purpose.

Chapter takeaway: Vulnerability is counter-intuitive. It doesn't make sense on the surface. But it is the path to a rewarding life. It doesn't just help us accomplish important things, but it allows us to be known and know others.

---

29. The Power of Vulnerability. (n.d.). Retrieved May 5, 2015, from https://www.ted.com/talks/brene_brown_on_vulnerability?language=en

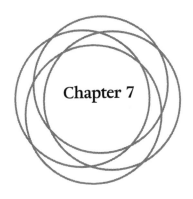

Chapter 7

Wired Networks:

Building High-Powered Groups and Teams

"Innovation—the heart of the knowledge economy—is fundamentally social."
— Malcolm Gladwell

What Malcolm Gladwell is telling us, Silicon Valley has shown us; innovation has a lot to do with the culture of the company and the quality of its relationships.

As I am writing this chapter, I am working with the chief operating officer of a successful technology company here in Los Angeles. In his words, the company needs to exceed their sales goals consistently. They also need a better environment for doing business. They need to optimize their culture.

Changing a Culture

How do we change or optimize a culture while keeping expectations high for performance and outcomes? Reed Hoffman is the co-founder of LinkedIn and author of several books. His latest effort is *The Alliance: Managing Talent in the*

Networked Age[30]. There, Reed does a fantastic job discussing how to build an optimized business culture, which I now refer to as the "culture of trust." He talks about integrating these four elements to change a culture:

1. Mutual Commitment
2. Mutual Investment. When an employee sees their personal mission and the company's personal mission as one.
3. Mutual Benefit. Both the employee and company feel, believe, and know that there is an equal amount of benefit for both of those entities in that relationship.
4. A framework that communicates the progress of this newly desired relationship and ensures that it's fulfilling the promise in both directions.

The opportunity to build high levels of trust in any organization creates electricity in people. It is a robust and unstoppable energy that transforms the work environment. It moves people into high gear and new levels of engagement and achievement. Silicon Valley has attracted the attention of the world by its example in this area.

I had the pleasure of introducing our company, The Performance Group, to an elite group of business leaders last June in Berlin, Germany. Berlin is now an epicenter for startups in that geographic region. As I began to explain to them that The Performance Group has adopted a blueprint to recreate

---

30. Hoffman, R. (2014). *The Alliance*. Boston, Massachusetts: HBR Press.

what is happening in Silicon Valley, they were all ears. They clearly admired what Silicon Valley has accomplished, and they esteemed Google CEO Eric Schmidt for creating this optimized business culture.

What have they done in Silicon Valley that the world is so intrigued by? In addition to making a lot of money, they have developed an aura and a business culture that even the Berliners admitted has not been created in successful German companies. This aura is the culture that Reed Hoffman speaks about. It is a culture that we love putting into practice at The Performance Group. It is value driven and centered on people and trust. It is this kind of culture that has taken companies like Google, Apple, and Amazon through the roof.

Now, I have a personal (humbling) example of the complete opposite. When I was a lieutenant in the United States Navy (1992-1995), we had the privilege of serving about four thousand aviators and aircrew members per year at our Aviation Physiology Training Unit. Our high-risk training facility had $2.4 million of equipment and a staff of 15. My job was to lead, inspire, and motivate our staff to hit our weekly goals while maintaining the highest levels of safety.

We worked hard all year, put up impressive numbers, and became number one in the country for most personnel trained.

As the lead division officer in 1994, I decided to host a holiday party for my staff. When I announced it, I told them that the party was "optional." The evening of the party was a shocker: Only 30 percent of my staff showed up. Why? It was because I was all about results at that time, and I hadn't invested in the relationships.

Most companies can put results over relationships and see some great short-term gains. In the long run, however, it creates a lot of dysfunction. As a leader in the Navy, I created a culture that won games, not championships. It was easier to focus on the short game and the quick fixes than to care about the lives and needs of the people I led. It was easier to push our people and be motivated by another ribbon for our chests.

Invest in People, Regardless

Companies and employees that build powerful groups and teams that bring exceptional results create a culture that has moved away from a hierarchal focus and toward a collaborative focus. It's not until the culture is rewired that the people will experience the power of the new vision and move from a traditional culture to an innovative culture.

The building of these high-power groups and teams centers on the vision and commitment of the C-Suite. A great post circulating through social media underscores this reality: The CFO of a company says to his CEO, "What if we train our people, and they leave?" The CEO responds to the CFO, "What if we don't, and they stay?" How do we invest in people without knowing what their real motives are and what they want to do? I'll talk more about that later in the following chapters.

Building High-Performance Relations

"What type of research does he have to support this...?" This was the question asked in my opening presentation in Berlin, Germany, at the Berlin Capital Club. I was invited to speak as an executive coach on the topic of culture optimization and why anyone should hire a coach to accomplish this. For a culture that high prioritizes structure, privacy, and punctuality, I was treading in new territory. I could hear Rodney Dangerfield's voice in the background saying, 'tough crowd, tough crowd."

Convincing the German people to do anything except continue to lead Europe's economy and make world-class cars can be intimidating. But as we wrapped up our informal discussion following the keynote address, several people spoke directly to me. They said these specific words: "I have never seen an authenticity and a willingness to connect in a business setting here in our culture." It felt like watching a home run ball sail over the fence at Fenway Park.

The Berlin Wall

The Berlin Wall is an iconic example of change and evolution, but it is also an excellent metaphor for relationships. Building great relationships comes from tearing down the walls that are obstacles to trust.

By the end of Day 2 in Berlin, I watched business leaders from Oracle, Siemens, Pay Pal, Otis Elevators, and Ricoh drop their guard and publicly say things they have never said. Here is how it happened:

I was transparent about myself. I was *vulnerable* with my hopes and desires, my family (I was told Germans aren't that), and my concerns about launching a company in their country.

1. I publicly esteemed our host, a local executive who invited me to speak. I took several minutes to discuss our friendship, our mutual passions, and our vision for the future together.
2. I told them up front that although I was presenting, I genuinely believed my reason for this visit was to learn from them about the German business culture and the German people. I also told them that I had a

deep respect for them. I said that it was a high honor to be able to not just address such a distinguished group of leaders, but also dialogue with them and learn from them.

3. In my presentation, I reminded them of universal truths that bound our cultures and countries together like the need to be relevant, effective, cared for, and personally growing.

4. As I presented my speech, I looked them directly in the eye and spoke with care, conviction, and sincerity.

5. In my preparation for the speeches, I took genuine care in wanting them to benefit. I was more concerned about their needs.

6. I left them with a takeaway lesson that I learned as an Officer in the Navy. The lesson was that you can't build a high-performance team by elevating performance over relationships. Invest in mutual relationships and the performance will follow. Interestingly, our German business leaders agreed.

There is an African proverb that says, "If you want to go fast, go alone. If you want to go far, go together." If we want to go far in business today, we have to learn how to go together. Create that culture, that magic, and we can change the game by creating a championship mindset.

Chapter takeaway: To rewire means to build a culture of trust – a blueprint for teams and groups that helps organizations develop a championship mindset.

Chapter 8

Complete Disconnect:

How to Rewire a Significant Relationship

"The real voyage of discovery consists not in seeking new landscapes, but in having new eyes."
— Marcel Proust

This chapter is all about how to rewire a badly damaged relationship, especially a significant one. It's about finding the "new eyes" that Marcel Proust suggests needed to look beyond the carnage of a painful relationship and toward this discovery: Not only can the relationship be rebuilt, but it can be rebuilt in a way far better than the failed first version.

The principles I present here can be applied to any professional or personal relationship. However, this chapter is specifically designed to repair, restore, and revive a badly damaged relationship that's significant to us.

After working with several hundred couples in this specific area, I found the most difficult piece to rewire is trust. I've watched couples forgive one another of egregious offenses, but reestablishing trust is the biggest challenge.

Whether or not you have faith in God or any particular religion, the biblical account of Adam and Eve and their downfall offers insights that are remarkable and timeless. It is interesting to note that they left an ideal situation. They were originally in a fairytale-like state, and they had what everyone is looking for. There was no pretense, no shame or guilt, just love. But then they crossed a line, and once they crossed over that line, they began to suffer.

What line did they cross? Eve lied; Adam blame shifted, and neither took responsibility.[31] That's perhaps the easiest card to play in most messed up relationships: "We are in this mess because of you." As soon as we go down that road, we look for relief and open the door to something outside of the relationship – a substitute instead of a solution.

What's the substitute? It is anything that distracts us from confronting the real issues. It could be work, recreation, alcohol, shopping, pornography, or illicit sexual experiences. Or it could be that sweet person that you are now slowly falling into a trance over. This person captivates you because she or he is doing what your spouse or someone competent should be doing; they are listening intently without judgment to all your aches and pains. Pick your poison. Any of them will destroy a damaged relationship that's still salvageable.

---

31. Henry, M. (2003). *Lessons from Adam and Eve.* Nashville, Tennessee: Thomas Nelson.

New Eyes

We restore trust by taking full responsibility and being honest. When we stop blaming and attacking, and we can start looking to make a bad situation good, it's amazing how the person in the cross hairs changes. Our hearts soften, and we find a new sense of self that's more heroic and admirable than the weak-willed whiner that always pulls out the victim card. We need to be honest about what we have and have not done to build a better relationship.

I love metaphors in life and how they become a foreshadowing of something with a hidden meaning we need to learn. Then we can look in the rear-view mirror and realize it wasn't a coincidence, but it was intended to get our attention and take action.

My foreshadowing event was the Northridge earthquake on January 17, 1994. It was measured at 6.7 in magnitude. Scientists from Cal Tech stated that the earthquake produced the strongest ground motions ever instrumentally recorded in an urban setting in North America.

At that time, my wife and I were living in San Clemente, California, and she was traveling on business. I was entertaining a friend from New York, and we were mostly playing tennis and surfing. The night before the earthquake, we over-indulged on Mexican food and margaritas. So when the earthquake hit, and my bed felt like it was standing up vertically at 4:30 am, I thought it was just an old friend playing a joke on me.

That earthquake was a foreshadowing of what came four months later. At that time, I had done many things right, but as a promising career officer in the United States Navy, I was facing a near divorce.

Deeply distressed and completely disconnected, my wife of seven years and I were bitter and planned our divorce. We tried traditional counseling and went to a practitioner who specialized in "breakthroughs." But we were cooked. Done. I found it absurd that some things in life had exceeded my expectations, yet my personal life was crumbling, irretrievable, and beyond my control to fix.

But then we went to a theatrical play hosted by a local church. We weren't looking for a church or Jesus; we were just looking for relief. However, soon after, we slowly and guardedly started to open up to others about our damaged relationship. We began to wrestle with the idea of forgiveness and the call to be completely honest with one another for the first time in our marriage. What followed was not expected.

After the pain of confessing to each another that we wandered out of our marriage, we both took full responsibility for how we failed each another. Much like quickly ripping off a 4 x 4-inch adhesive bandage, it was a "raw" feeling for the first several days. A supportive group of competent people and a new blueprint for change helped us through it. Through a painful and potent transformation that included changing my values, identifying my beliefs, and being brutally honest, I experienced a complete rewiring of the mind. I was able to move past the limiting beliefs that crushed my marriage, and I was capable of creating a far better marriage than conceivable.

Our badly damaged marriage was not just restored but rewired on a new platform of humility, forgiveness, and a desire to make things better. The result? We will celebrate our 28th wedding anniversary this fall – with a friendship and sex life that's far more rewarding than previously.

As a result of my transformation, I became more selfless in my relationships. I was able to help others create profound changes in *their* relationships. And for the first time in my life, I had a purpose. My eyes were open to helping others. And I knew my experiences in previous careers in science, aviation, and medicine would all play a pivotal role.

How Science Changed the field of Coaching

After my transformation, my calling was crystallized. I watched the field of neuroscience become a new frontier for personal development. I learned how the mind is capable of changing in a positive way when the right elements are in place. Changing (rewiring) the way they thought would bring power into their lives. It was magnetic. I realized that my calling was to create transformative experiences for people that would rewire their mind by uniquely applying the principles of neuroscience.

And that's what it means to be rewired and put power into relationships.

The Power of One

I once gave a testimonial speech at a seminar on rebuilding a badly damaged marriage (yes, mine!). I was the only male in the auditorium, with an attendance of about 500 women. I described my responsibility in weakening the marriage in a way that placed the burden and responsibility fully on me. It got very quiet. Seeing someone take full responsibility in a two-way commitment inspires confidence that change is possible.

Fortunately for my wife and me, we were both commit-ted to the pain of change. I know full well that sometimes only one person is committed while the other can't seem to muster the will to try again. Miraculously, what I have *also* witnessed is that when one person shifts their will to make it work "at all costs," even the most stubborn partner will turn and follow.

Adam and Eve used deceit to cover over their damaged friendship. It is the same deceit that we use today until we discover the eyes to navigate the damaged relationship. There is much hope when we enter into the pain of change – "the road less traveled."

It's easy to point fingers. However, anyone who's genuinely willing to look at themselves with the intention of taking ownership and changing themselves will find the relief they long for. That's because personal responsibility and ownership lead us to brokenness.

How We Change

Brokenness, or contrition, is a change of heart that follows a change in what we think and believe. This change is deep, lasting, and sensitizes us to how we've affected others. Brokenness from hurting someone else creates a desire to see justice done, even if it means a greater personal cost. [32] It's not merely an approach for change, it is a gift from God, also known as Metanoia.

Whoa, wait a minute! What if I don't believe in God – does this still work? Yes, it works because that's how we are designed to work. But sometimes we need a certain set of circumstances and a Sherpa to carry our stuff to make the steep climb toward change. It is virtue, altruism, and everything good all wrapped into one. But beware that it can get uglier before it gets better, and this route is not for the warm fuzzy crowd. This could be your Hillary Step.

---

32. Edwards, G. (1980). *A Tale of Three Kings*. Newnan, Georgia: Seed Sowers House.

Nine Steps to Restore Trust

1. Face the real issue. We have to be clear and careful about assessing and confronting the right issue. At times, it can seem black and white. For example, your spouse is struggling with pornography, and we are ready to throw the book at them. They are certainly guilty, but what if there are root issues on both sides of the marriage, and pornography was just the relief valve? If you don't kill the issue at the root, the weeds will grow back. A Sherpa that has a superior skill set in diagnosing relational issues should be called upon for a thorough assessment. It's difficult to restore trust in a relationship until we figure out what the core issue is.

2. Honesty. Being honest about yourself and restraining yourself from attacking and judging prematurely is high ground for rewiring a severely damaged relationship. Even if it seems difficult, you can do it. You are far stronger than your emotions tell you.

3. Take full responsibility. This opens the door to a higher level of thinking. This is not about who is right – it is about what was right. The high ground is often restoring a relationship that is badly damaged, and not abandoning it. Then we are no longer victims of poor parenting, bad circumstances, or any other excuse we can come up with. This is a game changer.

4. Strive for brokenness. This is when we get the new eyes that Marcel Proust talks about. When the heart changes, the eyes see things differently. This is "brokenness" – a spiritual principle that has the power to change the most difficult situations. It is that moment when a person becomes sorrowful for the right reason. They are not grieved because they were caught, or because it will cost a lot of money, or they will be shamed, or lose their reputation. They become sorrowful because they have wounded another person with their recklessness and carelessness. They realize that they have deeply hurt another human being. They now feel responsible to do whatever it takes to restore the relationship.[33]

5. It's what I do, not say. When someone has committed an offense, the offender must have the humility to *do* whatever it takes for the offended to believe they are changing and committed to a new way. The offender must be willing to be accepted on current and future activity, *not* promises. Don't just tell your partner what you intend to do, *show* them. Actions will speak volumes. In fact, the road back is less talk and more action.

There should be a period (undetermined time) where the offended party has a right to and should be privy to specific details about the offender's activities. Phone call logs, credit card purchases, and social media sources are all fair game. Until the relationship is restored, the offender has to get rid of the self-pity attitude of feeling judged, imprisoned, or micromanaged. If you blew it, own it. The offended party must know there are no boundaries to privacy because you

---

33. Edwards, G. (1980). *A Tale of Three Kings*. Newnan, Georgia: Seed Sowers House.

have nothing to hide. Only this level of commitment will remove all the suspicion and anger of the transgression. So stand firm in the new conviction that you will be judged on what you do, not what you say, and there are no "off-limits" until both parties feel restored.

6. Practice humility. Humility will have to become a new language. The new eyes that are opened are the eyes of the heart. Humility is the attitude that accomplishes this.[34]

Humility gives us the courage to express our needs and desires. When we commit to talking about things ranging from personal desires to money management to our sexual needs without attacking or judging each other, we position both parties in a way that opens the door to change.

7. Create new definitions and expectations. Creating new definitions and expectations is an incredibly potent tool for restoring a severely damaged relationship. I have seen clients receive tremendous relief just by taking the time to define parts of their lives such as marriage, love, sex, parenting, and financial freedom. I am amazed at how simple and powerful it is to define these areas and how it brings immediate and rewarding results.

For example, I was on the board of a hospital with a woman with whom there was a negative experience. In the same

---

34. Murray, A. (1982). *Humility*. New Kensington, Pennsylvania: Whitaker House.

way, my wife had a negative working relationship with a man. We both chose to honor each other by leaving those positions and relationships. We both found new convictions that clear boundaries were the pathway to restoring our marriage.

When both parties want to make the other feel respected and safe, trust is restored, and hope begins to bear new fruit. One of the most important things you could do in the phase of rebuilding trust is to pledge to remove anything that would make your partner feel awkward, disrespected, or insecure. I was once in the Caribbean as an actor on a commercial shoot for a national spot. The client put us all up in an exquisite resort. When my co-actress asked me to dinner, I thought about what my wife might think of me being alone at dinner with another woman in San Juan, Puerto Rico. I cordially declined. It's this type of definition that both parties need to feel great about to move on to new ground.

It might be yes to business dinners, but no business drinks afterward. In these matters, you have to find each other's comfort level and hold to it. It's counterintuitive, but it works. It's like taking off a tourniquet and reestablishing blood flow.

For some, this is a new way of living. To get good at it, I would recommend joining a support network. It could be, for example, a community group, a church, or a think tank. Evaluate the kind of friendships you have and how they influence your thinking. There have to be new expectations for a damaged relationship to be restored.

8. Redefine commitment. There are times when couples need to put into words their definition of being committed in the relationship. What does it mean to be faithful? What does it mean to be loyal? What does it mean to be sacrificial? What is a mutually enjoyable sex life look like? It would seem like a no-brainer, but very few people take the time to do it.

9. Gratitude. Gratitude is a profound tool for couples that are restoring trust and rebuilding commitment.[35] Put together a journal and write one or two specific things about your spouse that you are grateful for each day. Then set a time to talk to your spouse about these things. This is a life-giving tool.

These are nine steps to restoring trust and rebuilding commitment that have worked profoundly in my life and in the lives of hundreds of couples I've counseled and coached. These tools have had tremendous success in not just reviving but rewiring severely damaged relationships.

Chapter takeaway: We can rewire badly damaged relationships by restoring trust and renewing commitment. When we commit to these, we see old relationships with new eyes. It requires taking full responsibility and being completely honest. It's painful, but it produces extraordinary results. And don't do it alone; invite a Sherpa to carry what you can't.

---

35. Ferguson, G. (2000). *The Power of Gratitude*. Spring, Texas: Illumination.

Chapter 9

Hotspot:

Best Sex Ever

"The cave you fear to enter holds the key to your treasure."
— Joseph Campbell.

WARNING: THIS CHAPTER COULD REALLY HELP YOU

I wrote part of this chapter at Starbucks. Seated next to the sugar and creamer service, people would occasionally glance at my screen. One side was entitled Chapter 9: Best Sex Ever. The other part of the screen was my Safari browser entitled "regions of the brain that are active during sex." I know what they must have been thinking: "Man, this guy's a pervert – and in plain view!"

While it's clear that pharmacology (like Viagra) and companies like Victoria's Secret are bringing new life to old sex organs, the solution to our shortcomings in the sexual realm may lie elsewhere. It may be in the most overlooked sexual organ of all – the brain.

Neuroscience is now offering keys to the treasure chest for those who want to create new outcomes in the bedroom and "boldly go where no man (or woman) has gone before."

This chapter is about creating a more desirable sex life by rewiring our current thinking about sex and the steps to change it practically. It involves the following: Identifying our limiting beliefs about sex, verbalizing our sexual ideal, and understanding the role science may play in our sexuality.

Limiting Beliefs about Sex

After thousands of hours in marriage counseling, it has become apparent to me that we have a hard time talking about our sex lives – except when it comes to complaining about it. Men fear being rejected. Women fear being used. Because of the gridlock this creates, many new and exciting ideas go unexplored. We need a vocabulary to overcome the limiting beliefs from our sexual past and an approach that unlocks the treasure trove of unmitigated joys.

Many of us have a hard time (no pun intended) talking about mutual orgasms, five new ways to excite the clitoris, or bringing in a new gadget to extend the joys of our monogamy. And only the bravest will act out their fantasies together. It is the cave of fear that Campbell refers to in the quote above. We must enter this cave in order discover the treasure, which, in this case, is a mutually fulfilling sex life. We all have a past that frames our sexuality. Some have been fortunate, others less so. Many of us have experiences that create barriers or limiting beliefs in some area of our sexual lives.

Side note: If you have a physical limitation or believe you need professional help to untangle a painful past, go for it.

If, however, you are one of the millions of people who have just lost heart that it can be exciting (without it being illegal or unethical), read on; this is a game changer.

Let's identify some limiting beliefs about sex. Here is a short list of examples:

A. Too many stars have to align for it to be worth it
B. I feel too needy when I initiate too often
C. I get rejected too often when I initiate
D. It's just about fulfilling a need, not a Hollywood romance scene
E. I've got baggage, so it's complicated
F. I'm just too tired
G. With the job and raising kids, it's not a priority anymore
H. People in my station of life don't get very involved in this area
I. We're old, so I'm just not that into it anymore
J. The spirit is willing, but the flesh is weak (erectile dysfunction)

Limiting beliefs about our sex life can create unwanted emotions that crush desire or performance. Performance coaching offers a specialized way to remove limiting beliefs about our sexuality and create new ideals that move us toward a world full of unexplored treasures.

A New Teaching

As I mentioned, in 1994, hope was restored to our marriage, and a new foundation of trust opened the door to great sex. It was a total mind shift, which happened by removing limiting beliefs about sex and committing to pleasing each other.

We also received a new piece of information that shifted our view of sex. According to the Christian teaching about marriage, "your body is not your own."[36] Simply put, when one of you wants it, it is available without push back. This is about being available as often as necessary for one another sexually. This was balanced with the teaching that love and respect are the foundations to this agreement, not imposing a selfish will. Can you imagine the power *available* in marriage with this type commitment? And can you imagine how this would alter the statistics on adultery, divorce, and pornography?

Yes, this is rated R for mature audiences. It is a teaching that will send a shock wave through most couples' relationships. But for us, it was our Copernican moment that created something beautiful in our lives. Again, it was a Metanoia, a profound change in mindset or perspective.

Remember Henry Fords words, "Whether you think you can or think you can't, you are right." We too believed the wrong things about our relationship and sexuality. Your first step is to identify any limiting belief you have about sex. Then make the decision to remove it.

Verbalize Our Sexual Ideal

When men go unfulfilled in their sex lives, it quickly deteriorates into bitterness, promiscuous thinking, flirting, or pornography. It's a downhill slope from there to adultery

---

36. *Holy Bible, New International Version.* (2012). Grand Rapids, Michigan: Zondervan Bible.

and divorce. If a man doesn't learn how to navigate the issue well, he will be one of those guys drinking craft beer at the local brewery talking about the latest and greatest. But once he lowers his guard, he will tell you (with an edge in his voice) about the lack of sex in his married life. Gentlemen, if you're reading this chapter, here is the hard truth: We are more responsible for this than we will admit.

For a woman, if she cannot establish the emotional connection she needs to her man, sex becomes a chore. But here is the conundrum: A man needs to feel desired and know that his woman wants him, and a woman must *first* feel that her man cares and wants to protect her. This is a book in and of itself!

The first step in constructing an ideal is hopeful dialogue. It has to be gentle, nonjudgmental, non-accusatory, and filled with a Ron Howard type of altruism that makes even the most hardened cynic want to become a believer again. Yes, it requires a level of self-denial for some of us who have been drinking from the fountain of our favorite cable news channel. This is a new canvass that you get to paint on together, and it needs to be treated as a sacred space.

Next is the fun part: putting color on the canvas. It's talking, perhaps for the *first* time, about your ideal vision of giving and receiving intimately. Here are some basic ground rules: Ladies first.

1. Be specific about what you would want to give.
2. Be specific about what you would want to receive.

3. Every suggestion is to be considered without push back.

4. Any suggestion considered degrading or negative should be dismissed only after a fair discussion about it.

5. Each new idea should be experienced without a pass/fail approach and looked at as a "successful attempt" regardless of the outcome.

6. Discuss specific circumstances that diminish drive (kids can hear us, talking about problems in bed just prior to foreplay, etc.) and what you can do to overcome or avoid them.

7. Commit to identifying someone you mutually trust and respect to give input and feedback if there is a block.

An Example from an Unsuspected Source

Turning through the steamy pages of the Old Testament, we find Shulamith, who is one of the many wives of King Solomon. Shulamith is an example of the ideal sexual self.[37] She displays what most every couple is looking for. The attributes lead to a sexual experience that, when packaged together, are the dynamite that we are hoping to detonate on date night. Shulamith had five qualities that electrified their intimate life. She was responsive, adventurous, uninhibited, expressive, and sensuous. Here are two fun exercises that will allow you to explore these qualities together.

---

37. Dillow, J. (1977). *Solomon on Sex*. Nashville, Tennessee: Thomas Nelson.

Exercise 1: Explain in detail what it looks like and feels like to be sexually:

- Responsive
- Adventurous
- Uninhibited
- Expressive
- Sensuous

Exercise 2: Sketch the ideal sexual self or experience similar to Exercise 1. Use your own words, characters, or imagination. Let it run wild. This is a time to go big. Fear is to be expected in conquering new ground, but don't let fear discourage your progress.

Making it happen will take effort, and this is where the next step offers some insight into helping us change.

The Role of Science in Our Sexuality

Our sexual past is etched into our subconscious mind. Unlike a computer that records facts and data points, we store memories as a synthesis of different experiences, emotions, and facts.[38] If we could only change the facts (data) and connect this new information with new experiences (positive), we could create a more desirable landscape in our sexuality. Under certain conditions, our understanding of science can

---

38. Turrell, M. (2012, March 18). Sex and the Brain: How Neuroscience May Soon Change All Our Relationships. Retrieved May 5, 2015, from https://markturrell. wordpress.com/2012/03/18/sex-and-the-brain-how-neuroscience-may-soon-change-all-our-relationships-6/

help. If we can rewire our minds to stop smoking, we can rewire our minds for better sex.

The Intersection of Science and Sexuality

Love promises us a chest pounding, toe curling, lip snarling treasure of delight. But to open the treasure chest, you may need a key or two. Neuroscience offers us the keys to the treasure in the form of the hormones dopamine, serotonin, oxytocin and vasopressin. All of these play a key role and are delivered during the sexual experience.[39]

- Dopamine: pure pleasure, "fireworks."
- Serotonin: less potent cousin to dopamine, "afterglow."
- Oxytocin: it is what bonds us through pleasant and casual contact as well.
- Vasopressin: the "armored knight" of hormones whose role is to give us the courage to protect our object of desire to the death – literally.

These hormones are only released when certain parts of the brain are activated during arousal. Serge Stoleru and his colleagues from the CERMEP have identified five specific areas of the brain that are activated during arousal. These five areas are the inferior temporal cortex, the right orbitofrontal cortex, the left anterior cingulate cortex, the right insula, and the right caudate nucleus.[40]

---

39. Turrell, M. (2012, March 18). Sex and the Brain: How Neuroscience May Soon Change All Our Relationships. Retrieved May 5, 2015, from https://markturrell. wordpress.com/2012/03/18/sex-and-the-brain-how-neuroscience-may-soon-change-all-our-relationships-6/

40. Brain Mapping Of Sexual Arousal. (1999, February 23). Retrieved May 5, 2015,

How can we connect the science to the sex?

1. Identify and remove our limiting belief.
2. Identify positive new words attached to each specific component of sex (body image, phase of sex, desire, outcome).
3. Create the ideal in your mind. Meditate and welcome the positive emotions associated with it.
4. Engage as many of the senses as possible (perfume, music, candles, water, light, bedding, etc.) to further establish the wanted thoughts and match them to the desired emotions.

How can we connect neuroscience further with these practical steps? Our friends from Lumosity reminded us earlier[41]: When we create opportunities to explore our sexuality that are novel, adaptive and complete, we open the door to developing new circuitry in the brain. This might not sound sexy, but it is.

Final Thoughts

By intentionally combining new data (thoughts) and new experiences in our sexuality, we can recreate a sexuality that is adventurous, uninhibited, and expressive. Going forward, we have the ability to change our views and our experiences.

---

from http://www.scienceagogo.com/news/19990123232858data_trunc_sys.shtml

41. Neuroscience 101: A guide to your amazing brain. (n.d.). Retrieved May 22, 2015, from http://www.lumosity.com/

This is what it means to be *Rewired*. This is where sex becomes even more fulfilling.

Committing to changing the way you think personally about your sexuality can also be a potent platform to conquering other issues. Take hold of the treasure of intimacy. It is a gift, and applying these principles and steps can get us there.

When confronted with a limiting belief about achieving the ideal, we can do the following:

1. Discuss openly the thoughts and feelings connected to the limitation (limiting belief).
2. Agree to talk to someone who is qualified to help change this way of thinking.
3. Commit to changing the way you think about the subject and view this obstacle as a new platform for other issues and take hold of the gift of the treasure of intimacy.
4. Agree to experience the ideal mutually without judgment.
5. Enjoy the journey and give each other permission to laugh along the way.

Chapter takeaway: Our intimate lives offer a treasure trove of unexplored experiences. On the other side of fear and limiting beliefs, we can grab hold of the treasure. We have to decide to use the keys and unlock the doors.

Part 3

Purpose

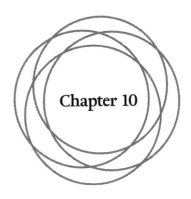

Chapter 10

Alternative Power:
Moving from Egotism to Altruism

"Virtue is its own reward and brings with it the truest and highest pleasure."

– John Henry Newman

Whether we frame the discussion in philosophy, religion or just common sense, anytime someone displays an unselfish regard for the welfare of others, there is a reward that's "highest and truest." Call it altruism or call it virtue. It is simply uncommon for most to operate in a selfless way. Why is selflessness such a struggle?

Other than opening a door, picking up something from the ground that someone dropped, or sending an occasional greeting card, we haven't been schooled to think about others *first*. It's a paradox. It's counterintuitive.

According to author David F. Wells, it is because we live in a culture that has fundamentally shifted away from character and toward personality. This shift has "spawned an industry obsessed with self: self-image, self-ideal, the true and false self, inner self, and self-actualization."[42] Not to mention a culture of "selfies."

There is another alarming aspect of this trend regarding the focus on self.

Sociologist John Rice has noted that the United States has half the world's clinical psychologists, up from 12,000 in 1968 to 42,000 in 1990. We have one third of the world's psychiatrists. In the fifteen years between 1975 and 1990, clinical social workers increased by 320 percent and family counselors by 680 percent.[43]

Moving from Egotism

In 1994, when my paradigm shifted from serving myself to serving others, it was like that scene in the *Wizard of Oz* when it went from black and white to color. I was giddy with the newfound reality that I could care more about the interests of others without sounding off the self-preservation alarm. It created a revival of spirit that led me to 17 years of full-time service in the Christian ministry. How? It was an inside job: a rewiring of the mind. In an overly simplified way, I moved from egotism to altruism.

---

42. Wells, D. (1998). *Losing our Virtue: Why the Church Must Recover Its Moral Vision*. Grand Rapids, Michigan: W.B. Eerdmans.

43. Wells, D. (1998). *Losing our Virtue: Why the Church Must Recover Its Moral Vision*. Grand Rapids, Michigan: W.B. Eerdmans.

What Are We Talking About?

In this chapter, we are identifying a simple strategy to 1) make self-centered pursuits more other-centered or 2) pursue future goals that have a higher altruistic value.

How This Works Practically

It is highly rewarding to help others move from self-interest to altruistic motivation. First, we evaluate significant goals and accomplishments, and we begin to pull apart what is driving them. We discuss how the ego may be driving our ambition, as well as how unmet needs drive ambition. Next, we do a simple exercise that identifies our top 5 values. From there, we discuss how these values are active in our day-to-day lives. Then we begin to identify specific values and elements of altruistic living that can be attached to the goal (table below). For example, having someone shift their ambition from needing to feel superior to wanting to build a high performing team is exhilarating.

Egotism	Altruism
Self-interest	Charity
Self-admiration	Affection
Greed	Social conscience
Superiority	Teamwork
Conceit	Praise of others

In a similar way, shifting your motive from being number one to mentoring others will not only reap personal rewards, but will also build a culture of high performers.

Alternative Power

At the time of writing this book, billionaire technocrat Elon Musk announced that his electric car company, Tesla, is planning to change the way people power their homes.

In a tweet last month, Musk announced that Tesla would be unveiling a new product on April 30. This new product is a $13,000 battery that "could keep your home online in a blackout."[44]

Similarly, we can change the way we power our ambitions and tap into this alternative source. Any of us who look for a second wind to accomplish our next great venture needs to look no further than the power of helping others. Altruism,

44. Preston, B. (2015, April 25). Retrieved May 5, 2015, from http://www. theguardian.com/technology/2015/apr/25/tesla-battery-home-elon-musk

the intentional pursuit of helping others ahead of self, is the road less traveled. It is an alternative power source that allows us to see the world with a fresh set of eyes and to fuel your efforts to the next level.

We can rewire our motivation to achieve future ambitions and reap meaningful rewards by:

1. Evaluating our goals and the sources of motivation
2. Looking at how values and unmet personal needs drive ambition
3. Identifying limiting beliefs toward altruism
4. Creating a new paradigm from a new discovery
5. Crafting a next achievement where others benefit
6. Anchoring changes through repetition or application

At The Performance Group, we offer one, two, or three-day immersions as well as 90 and 180-day packages to accomplish this process. We help rewire the goal and the rewards by moving away from ego (self) and toward altruism and satisfying the needs of others.

Chapter takeaway: When our clients leave egotism for altruism, they find an alternative power source for their personal ambitions and motivation. Sometimes they do the same thing with a different view, other times they discover something entirely different that strikes a cord. Either way, it becomes an alternative, renewable source of power. I have personally seen it work in the lives of hundreds of people. It has become one of the foundational pieces in my performance coaching practice.

Chapter 11

Power Bundle:

Adventure, Mission, and Romance

> *"A man is not old until regrets take the place of his dreams."*
>
> – John Barrymore

This quote is a warning to us all: don't get cynical, consider every opportunity and pursue your dreams. When people ask me about The Performance Group, I invariably quote Mark Twain and tell them plainly that we help people avoid the regrets that come when we pass up opportunities and give up on hope. We want them to tell their story, imperfect as it is, with gratitude and a hope for the future.

Some of us are just starting the second quarter. We are in our 30s, the world is our oyster, and we are charging hard! Others are coming out of halftime in our 40s and are planning on a fantastic second half. Some of us feel stuck in halftime[45], waiting for the rousing speech or the divine

---

45. Buford, B. (2001) *Stuck in Halftime: Reinventing Your One and Only Life.* Grand Rapids, Michigan: Zondervan Publishing House.

moment to get us running out the door and back to the playing field. And that's the goal of this chapter: to jumpstart the heart and pull us back into the expectation of what is possible.

It Starts with the Heart

"Cor" in Latin means "heart."[46] King Solomon tells us in Proverbs 4:23, "Above all else, guard your heart, for it is the wellspring of life."[47] It is the wellspring of life, the central source of living.

When I say it starts with the heart, I am not implying it starts with your emotion – not the rousing motivational speech that gives us a temporary kick in the pants. I mean it starts with the "Why." It is intended to uncover the meaningful thoughts and beliefs you already hold. Discover this, and the desired emotions will follow.

When we look at Madison Avenue, Hollywood, and Big Pharma, they are waging a valiant effort to keep both the imagination and the wallet open. They know that once men push past 40 and enter the second half of life, most of them are determined (some even desperate) to make the most of it. They are telling us that our heart loses its fire because our hair is thinning, our private parts are flailing, and our belly

---

46. Cord,cour,cor & court are the root-words for many other words. (n.d.). Retrieved May 5, 2015, from http://www.english-for-students.com/cord.html

47. *Holy Bible, New International Version.* (2012). Grand Rapids, Michigan: Zondervan Bible.

is protruding. They make no mention of the true source of the fire: the heart.

"Deep in his heart, every man longs for a battle to fight, an adventure to live, and a beauty to rescue."[48]

At The Performance Group, we look to the subconscious mind for clues about how to fulfill this quote. In the conscious mind, we find rational thinking. In the subconscious, we find imagination, intuition, and belief – the stuff that dreams are made of.

Whether it's the need to feel relevant or powerful or discover your calling, this chapter provides practical insights and steps to bundle key ingredients necessary to accomplish it. I've been fortunate to work with the Navy's elite. I've been a keynote speaker at international conferences, traveled the world as a product ambassador, and have been featured in television commercials that personify men who have made good decisions and aged well.

Was there a common theme? Yes. There are three elements that when bundled together create an extraordinary and powerful life. "Power Bundle" is about three elements that when activated become a potent force for good. They are Adventure, Mission, and Romance.

---

48. Eldredge, J. (2001) *Wild at Heart: Discovering the Passionate Soul of a Man.* Nashville, Tennessee: Thomas Nelson.

The Total Package

It is admirable when a man is adventurous, fit, and still takes risks as he is aging. When this *same* person pursues a mission or a higher purpose, it's remarkable. But when that same person has a *great* relationship with their significant other? Well, that person is a phenom – an icon – a man who all men look to and want to be. He's the total package.

What does this man offer? More than intrigue, he offers substance. He is a living hope for our future. We all marvel at a man like this because it is who we want to be, and who women want to be *with*. And it's a future that we want to experience.

Spend Money on Experiences, Not Things

The following excerpt is from a recent article by Fast Company entitled "The Science of Why You Should Spend Your Money on Experiences, Not Things."

There's a very logical assumption that most people make when spending their money: that because a physical object will last longer, it will make us happier for a longer time than a one-off experience like a concert or vacation. According to recent research, it turns out that assumption is completely wrong.

So rather than buying the latest iPhone or a new BMW, Gilovich suggests you'll get more happiness spending money on experiences like going to art exhibits, doing outdoor activities, learning a new skill, or traveling. [...]

'By shifting the investments that societies make and the policies they pursue, they can steer large populations to the kinds of experiential pursuits that promote greater happiness,' write Gilovich and his coauthor, Amit Kumar, in their recent article in the academic journal Experimental Social Psychology.[49]

Adventure – You Are Not Too Old

We have a legitimate need for mystery or discovery. Call it uncertainty or variety – but it all points toward activities that meet our need for adventure. But here is the hard truth: Many men shrink back from adventure because they have abandoned themselves. They have given in to excuses. Some have shipwrecked themselves, their families, and their jobs because they have not met this legitimate need. Instead, they have come up with a destructive alternative: overworking, laziness, gambling – it comes down to avoidance. Men go into hiding when they are not honest with themselves about this need, and that's why this chapter is critical.

I have a friend who is 62 years old. He is still club racing motorcycles. I've watched him take his Yamaha R1 to the racetrack and bend his bike into a chicane corner at Auto

---

49. The Science Of Why You Should Spend Your Money On Experiences, Not Things (n.d.). Retrieved May 5, 2015, from http://www.fastcoexist.com/3043858/world-changing-ideas/the-science-of-why-you-should-spend-your-money-on-experiences-not-thing

Club Speedway at well over 100 miles per hour. Every time he gets off his bike, it takes everything in me not to hug this guy. Why? Because he is a symbol: He is the embodiment of a man who is still taking the right risks. I watched him crash his motorcycle last year at a different racetrack. When we got back to the pit area, there were no complaints. Most men half his age would have cursed the sky if they fell off a curb and hit the ground, let alone crash a motorcycle. Not him.

Men love being around guys like him. Guys like him don't quit. They don't give in. They don't give up. They hold desperately to their sense of adventure, especially in the presence of achy backs, work challenges, and naysayers who tell them that it is selfish and reckless to have this part in their life. It's inspiring. It's a blast when you have a group of like-minded souls committed to living adventurously. We need a band of brothers.

Form a secret society. Each year, around eight of us meet to ride motorcycles in a different part of the U.S. Before you call it a glorified fraternity or a men's moto movement, there's more to the story: this is a club forged in values. Each of us loves bikes, but we love our family and our faith even more. And we cherish the friendships in the group. Yes, we treat it like an underground society. Yes, we have a private on-line location where source critical information is exchanged on a need-to-know basis. And yes, you can only get entrance and a secret clearance from the Commandant. We also have rituals (we banter about committing to the date and location, everyone gets a nickname, we ride in certain

formations, and we expect everyone to wear all their gear).
The expectation is to ride hard, ride safe, and be gentlemen
– do nothing that would be undignified. Most of our code-
of-conduct stems from our mutual faith.

What begins as a complaint session about achy backs and
family struggles finds its crescendo in laughter, stories of
close calls, and buckets of gratitude for a brotherhood that
most others are still struggling to find.

You are not too old for a secret society – or incapable of
finding one. If you are around people who think otherwise,
take a temporary break from them. Go find a group of people
who are doing interesting stuff, even if it's not a perfect
alignment. Go and explore. Take a risk, find a website, go
to a local bike shop, or ask your friends on Facebook. For
fun, write a bucket list – even if you think you are too
young for that kind of thing. But for the love of Pete, move

toward people who are taking the right risks. If you can't find a group, form one. People want what you want; all that's needed is a catalyst. Be the catalyst. And contact us if you want us to facilitate it on your behalf.

Mission – "That Others May Live"

Here is a confession: When I turned 40, I wanted to go back into the military. At the time, there was no midlife crisis or troubles in my personal or professional life. I just still wanted to "run with the bulls." So in a moment of midlife indiscretion, I applied for a position as a combat rescue officer in the United States Air Force. *Denied.* I was too old for a position in Special Operations. Even though my pectorals were still relatively chiseled, and I could run 10 kilometers in less than 42 minutes. Ouch. But what stuck with me was their motto: "That others may live."[50] Four potent words that drive the point home: We exist for you. These words have become the bedrock for helping others at The Performance Group.

How can we discover our mission? One way is to consider our values and align them with the direct benefit of others. And how does that work? Here is one example.

Value	Resource	Pace Setter Organization	Underserved Community
Belonging	Motorcycles	Wounded Warrior	Veterans of War

---

50. USAF PARARESCUE | That Others May Live (n.d.). Retrieved May 5, 2015, from https://www.pararescue.com/

That others may live. Doing what we love to do and using what we have to help someone else benefit has value.

I left the military to go into the ministry for this reason: I wanted to be a catalyst for good to overcome evil. It was that simple. I lived out this paradigm (below). Each time I met with an individual or couple, this was the filter I ran in every appointment, and it was energizing:

Evil	Good
Bitterness	Forgiveness
Leaving	Weaving
Tolerance	Love
Separation	Resolution

Romance – but Wait, There's More

The third and final element of the bundle is romance. The word romance can mean different things, but most agree it has something to do with heightened acts or expressions of love or affection between two people. But wait, there's more. Merriam-Webster defines the origin of the word romance as follows:

1. Marked by the imaginative or emotional appeal of what is heroic, adventurous, remote, mysterious, or idealized
2. Marked by expressions of love or affection
3. Someone who is not realistic or practical: someone who thinks that things are better or more exciting than they are in reality.

Borrowing from Merriam-Webster's definition, romance is not confined to an intimate act between two people. There are other facets: one is a mystery, and the other is the concept of an "ideal." Romance could be:

- Looking at the rings of Saturn for the first time last summer through a high-powered telescope in Canada
- Paddling out in large surf and listening to the sound transmitted through the water from the rocks, and small boulders being dragged across the ocean floor
- Standing at the top of a black diamond ski run after a fresh fall of snow at 7 am and being the first skier down a run where no one has yet laid ski tracks.
- Riding a motorcycle through Zion National Park and being floored by the pink hues of jagged rocks contrasted against a pale blue sky while listening to classical music
- Men on horseback driving livestock across remote parts of the interior; single-minded, rugged and re-sourceful

Here's the good news: We don't need to agonize over not having a "lover" to be in love – or to be romantic. We need a mystery to pursue, an ideal to create. One of the Adven-ture-Mission-Romance exercises we offer at The Performance Group helps clients identify what they are searching for. It's a simple tool to get people thinking about how to configure an approach to pursuing an ideal, a mystery, or an adventure.

Earth	Sea	Activity	Configured	Mode
Mountains	Ocean	Physical	Alone	Foot
Desert	Bay	Spiritual	Significant Other	2 Wheel
Forest	River	Intellectual	One other	4 Wheel
Plains	Lake	Visceral	Group	Other

Personal Example

When I proposed to my wife Julie, the whole experience was electric. I found a small restaurant in Connecticut on an airport runway that was a renovated opera house. I called ahead and set the menu. For dessert, I asked that each of us would be served a pint of Ben & Jerry's New York Super Fudge Chunk still in the carton (that was our thing back then). I still remember their white gloves holding the red containers on fine china. I had a dozen sterling roses there waiting for her.

The coolest part was getting there. Since it was 50 nautical miles in a straight line over the Long Island Sound by plane, I hired a Cessna to take us. But first we had several glasses of champagne and chocolate covered strawberries overlooking Long Island Sound before we boarded. She had no idea we were going to fly that evening since I told her dinner was local. It was a home run.

We Don't Have to Wait

There is more for us *now*. If you are single, you don't have to be hung up waiting for the ideal partner to experience romance. Instead, immerse yourself in what is mysterious; pursue your ideal. Don't let being alone stop you. "Leap, and the net will appear."[51] But if you have a partner, have this discussion about Adventure, Mission, and Romance. When these are bundled, it ignites the heart and unleashes power.

---

51. John Burroughs

The power bundle is the CPR that can save a man (or woman) from a premature death – from being at home romanticizing *about* life. When dreams die, so do ambition and imagination. Our only alternative is a false solution, which at best is weak, and at worst is destructive. That's when middle-aged men begin to abandon their ideals and common sense that gets them into trouble.

Put nitro and glycerin together, and it explodes. Put Adventure, Mission, and Romance together, and you have a silver bullet. It's a combination that, when properly balanced in a man's life, produces an outrageous result.

At the Performance Group, here's what we do: We partner with clients to create this power bundle to help people dream about the second half of life.

Here is how:

1. We identify your AMR or your Adventure, Mission Romance profile*. It is a series of exercises, tools, and conversations that are specific to the client. We come up with a profile that not just resonates with the client but ignites them.
2. Once we have the profile, we align the profile with an experience for the client(s).
3. We identify individuals or groups that are leaders with similar interests to create potential partners or future crossover opportunities.
4. We create a follow-up experience with likeminded people for other growth opportunities.

We accomplish these steps one-on-one or with a group. We also offer a weekly follow-up focus group for accountability if desired.

Chapter takeaway: When the heart dies, so does ambition and imagination. Adventure, Mission, and Romance is the power bundle that ignites the heart again and gets us dreaming for the second half of life. When these three elements are living and active, we avoid the pitfalls of destructive substitutes and create a wave of energy that sustains the pursuit of our dreams.

*The A-M-R profile is unique to The Performance Group.

Chapter 12

Unlimited Coverage:
Rewiring Faith, Religion, and Spirituality

> *"Just as a candle cannot burn without fire,*
> *men cannot live without a spiritual life."*
> — Buddha

> *"When I admire the wonders of a sunset or*
> *the beauty of the moon, my soul expands in the worship of the creator."*
> — Gandhi

> *"The thief comes only to steal and kill and destroy.*
> *I have come that they might have life, and have it to the full."*
> — Jesus of Nazareth

I was once in Lake Tahoe, Nevada and caught a rare glimpse of a celestial occurrence that makes it possible to see the sun rising and the moon setting simultaneously. The event is called a Selenelion, and it occurs when the sun and moon are 180 degrees apart in the sky at the same time.[52] Many of us have witnessed similar events that we would describe

---

52. Rouan, R. (2014, October 8). Sunrise, moonset - see both at once early Wednesday. Retrieved May 5, 2015, from http://www.dispatch.com/content/stories/local/2014/10/07/sunrise-moonset--see-both-at-once.html

as magical, sacred, or surreal. These are moments that our heart and soul register as unique, uncommon, or once in a lifetime occurrence.

When I came to faith in God, I had a similar experience. My faith "conversion" wasn't an emotional moment where I laid my hand on the altar or was moved by a vision in a poltergeist moment. It was instead a potent and painful examination of truth and consequences in scripture that culminated in the realization of Gods grace and forgiveness. It drew me to the love of God and rewired my heart and mind permanently.

It felt majestic, rare and extraordinary. For me, the curtain was peeled back. What I experienced for the first time as a Christian was also a group of highly diversified people united in love, forgiveness, inspiration, and commitment.

What followed this transition from worldliness into utopia was a three-year period of Camelot with unimaginable amounts of victories, friendships, stories of overcoming, and the like. It was a veritable love fest.

Then, about six years into my devotion to God and church, there began a period of internal conflict between me and other leaders. Through a series of disappointments, misplaced expectations, and maturing convictions about faith and church culture, I found myself in a different place spiritually. Although this part of my spiritual journey was painful, it deepened my convictions for God, His scripture, and His plan for my life. Haruki Murakami's quote "Pain is inevitable – suffering is optional" came to mind frequently.

This chapter is not about finding faith but restoring it. It's not about who's right. It's about what's right. Specifically, it is about untangling the disappointment and hurt that come from our choices as well as the choices of others as we together follow a system of faith. My intention is to help others who have had similar challenges or are currently struggling with their faith experience.

For the simplicity of this chapter, we will broaden our use of the word "faith." It will encompass all terms including God, spirituality, religion, church, temple, spiritual being, higher power, or a god of our own understanding.

A God of Your Own Understanding

As we look at the concepts of faith, religion, and spirituality, it's good to look at the statistics. According to the World Factbook, as of 2013, we had a world population of a little over seven billion people. Christianity comprised 33 percent of that population. The Muslim faith made up 23 percent and the Jewish faith 0.2 percent. Interestingly enough, only a little over 10 percent of the world would consider themselves either non-religious or atheist. Based on the above data, almost nine out ten people believe in some form of faith, religion, or spirituality.[53]

A perfect faith is made up of imperfect people. Any cursory read of the Bible will tell you that disagreement and conflict

---

53. (n.d.). Retrieved May 5, 2015, from https://www.cia.gov/library/publications/the-world-factbook/geos/xx.html

are common in religious communities. However, if challenges within the religious community are mishandled, it is easy to question the goodness of God based on the imperfections of man. Consequently, many of us will experience a significant letdown along the way in our spiritual journey and can be tempted to abandon our faith.

Pain That Brings Change

As I mentioned, my personal experience with conflict in my spiritual community came about six years into it. It was centered mostly on matters in the Bible that were loosely defined, referred to biblically as disputable matters.[54] These areas included church culture issues as well as leadership style. Other examples of ambiguous areas can include how many times a week to meet, how to distinguish unity in the faith from conformity to a leader's wishes, and best practices in processes to resolve conflict. There are many other situations where the Bible is silent, and we are left to harmonize and fill in the empty spaces with our best efforts.

In the Christian community, when people give advice without having a full understanding of scripture and the practical application, they can easily cause unnecessary damage. It can also happen that followers who disagree with the leadership in non-biblical or disputable matters are labeled as prideful or independent. That would mean, "they are not in step with

---

54. Romans 14:1. *Holy Bible, New International Version.* (2012). Grand Rapids, Michigan: Zondervan Bible.

the Spirit,"[55] meaning they are willful and not listening to the advice of "godly people who were put into their life to help them make best choices."

Leaders of religious organizations can mistakenly use their authority to have their personal agendas followed. At times, it will take a mature second party to discern these distortions, untangle the half-truths, and define a clearer representation of the faith from the teachings.

Love in Any Language

In Proverbs 27:5-6, it says, "Better is open rebuke than hidden love. The wounds of a friend can be trusted, but an enemy multiplies kisses."[56] This particular passage is a key tenant in a strong religious community. In essence, it says that if I care, I'm going to say the hard things to you. It is a very powerful teaching that I believe deeply and continue to practice. And here is the other side of the coin, or the Yin to the Yang: Sometimes the truth hurts. Sometimes love is tough. And sometimes character requires far more pain and inconvenience than we are willing to endure to gain it. You have to be careful not to shoot the messenger when it's the message you have a problem with. The serenity prayer is a great fallback: Change what you must; accept what you cannot change, and find the wisdom to know the difference.

---

55. Galatians 5:25. *Holy Bible, New International Version.* (2012). Grand Rapids, Michigan: Zondervan Bible.

56. Proverb 27. *Holy Bible, New International Version.* (2012). Grand Rapids, Michigan: Zondervan Bible.

Trust God, Love People, Don't Confuse the Two

Many who have lost hope in their spiritual community do not need to lose hope in their faith. Prayers can go unanswered, our noble deeds unnoticed, and our hopes unfilled. Worst of all, in a time of need, we may have an experience that becomes manipulative or even abusive. Even goodhearted people can twist the meaning of a text out of ignorance. At the end of the day, all of these yield the same result: We get hurt, and we lose heart. It can take months and sometimes years to recover. But there is hope. It can be rewired. You can learn to trust your faith above the pitfalls of man's misguided efforts.

Rewiring Your Faith

As a marriage and family minister for 17 years, I've watched people turn from destructive, hopeless situations to taking action on a new vision for life. I've watched marriages heal. I've watched relationships be restored. I've worked with Navy Seals on marital intimacy. I have helped ex-professional football players restore their personal integrity. I've helped surgeons overcome arrogance. I've watched scripture bring fighter pilots to immediate and complete humility. I've helped a Marine Corps reconnaissance diver find forgiveness and come to a rewarding faith. I've worked with a cross-section of many different types of people. I've seen more of the good, profound and sacred than I've seen of the other side. I have also helped people transition from controlling and manipulative situations by helping them develop proper boundaries and appropriate obedience to leaders and their expectations.

How can we rewire our precious faith and restore hope in this critical area? I've outlined 11 steps modified from Mary Alice Chrnalogars' book, *Twisted Scriptures*[57] to help us get there.

1. Separate human error from divine retribution. It is a liberating conversation that requires someone who's qualified such as an additional trusted religious leader, a therapist, or a specialized coach.

2. Better understand your primary needs. This is a cornerstone service offering at The Performance Group. If you don't understand your primary needs, you run the risk of having those needs met in ways that are unfavorable or even destructive.

3. Restore relationships to good people who are outside the bad experience.

4. Strengthen your trust in your personal decision-making, which can come from clarifying your values.

5. Disengage from any leadership structure that's threatened by your tough questions. That's a huge red flag.

6. Better understand your boundaries and appropriate levels of transparency.

7. Redefine terms, clarify meanings, and put scripture and your faith back into context. It has an immediate transformative power to renew our sense of faith.

8. Extend forgiveness. Forgive yourself first. It is one of the most powerful actions on this entire list. Although you can forgive someone, that doesn't mean that you have to trust him or her. Trust is something that's

57. Chrnalogar, M. (2000) *Twisted Scriptures: Breaking Free from Churches that Abuse.* Grand Rapids. Michigan: Zondervan Publishing House.

earned, not granted automatically.

9. Grieve the loss of the ideal. A faith-based experience is supposed to be rewarding. If it was a negative experience, it needs to be grieved just like you would grieve the loss a loved one.

10. Get away from a religious experience that has more to do with rules and checklists, and pursue a faith that liberates you from your bondage. But remember that challenges and personal battles will always need to be confronted and overcome for character and rewards to follow.

11. Pursue relationships and organizations that foster personal growth and development and lead to fulfilling your purpose and contributing richly to the lives of others.

Lastly, trust in God. Learning to trust God again is difficult and will take time.

One of the leaders in the Christian community who stands out to help us is Henry Cloud. In his book, *Changes That Heal*[58], Henry offers us this simple three-part reminder when it comes to rewiring your faith:

1. **Grace** is an unconditional acceptance where there is a freedom to be who you are on the way to who you want to become. If someone is to heal and move to the next level, they will need to feel like someone is going to catch them when they fall.

2. **Truth**. If grace is the safe, loving relationship, then the truth is what keeps us on the course like a compass.

---

58. Cloud, H. (1992). *Changes That Heal: How to Understand Your Past to Ensure a Healthier Future.* Grand Rapids. Michigan: Zondervan Publishing House.

It's the guardrail that keeps us from going off the road and crashing. As much as we need grace, we need the truth.

3. **Time.** As we untangle our issues and allow people back into our lives again, we need time for grace and truth to do its work. We also need someone in our lives reminding us not to demand a harvest until the season has come to produce the fruit of its work. This takes time.

Although it was painful and challenging, the hardship I've described led me to what I call a second transformative process. I had to take the power out of the rituals, culture, and hands of men and put that power back into God. It meant untangling and dismantling some distorted ideas about my allegiance to leadership and church and having a healthy obedience to a loving God. It meant leaving a rule-based religion for a mysterious, majestic and romantic God.

Chapter takeaway: We can make a heroic comeback from bad religion. Take the risk and reconcile the wounds of the past with someone who specializes in it. If we do this, we will again see with the eye of our heart, the rewards of a spiritual realm that will make us feel alive again. Walk in the presence of a supreme being who controls everything and offers unlimited coverage and a promise that whatever happens on Earth has a purpose. It is not accidental; it is engineered for this life and the life beyond. Let go of the pain and reach out for a God who is mysterious, majestic and romantic.

Part 4

Supplement

Chapter 13

Streaming Live in HD:
How to Make Change Stick

> *"Habit is a cable; we weave a thread of it each day,*
> *and at last we cannot break it."*

> – Horace Mann

Seeing in HD for the First Time

We bought our first High Definition TV about 11 years ago. At that time, our daughters were young, so when I invited my father over to show off the new 50-inch HD TV, the feature length film was *Finding Nemo*. I remember my father's expression when he saw the quality of the picture that evening. He was as riveted as anyone who watched Neil Armstrong lower himself down the ladder to walk on the Moon from Apollo 11.

A significant shift in our thinking is like seeing high definition imaging for the first time. We feel like we see something clearer than ever, and it's exciting. *The challenge, however, is sustaining the change.* To do so, we need to put into place a process to reinforce change and F.O.C.U.S. Otherwise, we run the risk of returning to our familiar ways.

Here is our four-part approach to rewiring new habits and sustaining change:

1. Tell Your Story

Once we have cleared away the limiting beliefs and claimed our liberating beliefs, it's time to change our story and tell it with a new courage and authenticity. We do this by writing a *new narrative* – and it is one of the most pivotal parts of making change stick. Writing your new narrative includes

1. Explaining the "Why."

2. Defining the Pathos, Ethos, and Logos in your story.

3. Integrating your values and new beliefs.

4. Integrating relevant experiences.

5. Telling the story with courage and vulnerability.

When we combine these pieces of content with new liberating beliefs to empower your new story, it's a game changer

2. Anchor Change in Experience

Up to this point, we have spoken about how science, data, and measurement play a role in change. However, our emotions and our body movement play a powerful role in helping us remember what we've learned. This is why experiential learning scenarios that involve movement are so potent. When we take a client to the racetrack, and their focus on an issue is combined with operating a car at high speed, it leaves an indelible imprint on their mind. In the same way, we encourage clients to engage in role-playing, improvisation, and any other form of playacting. This engages more senses and emotion, releases more hormones (like Oxytocin), and creates stronger neural networks that lead to lasting change.

3. Create a New Routine

The next step involves establishing a new routine that includes (but is not limited to) visualization, meditation, prayer, martial arts, and theta wave activity exercises. These new routines build a scaffolding that supports changed thinking.

4. Relax and Recover

Sustained high-energy output has to be balanced with relaxation and recovery. Hard-working athletes need a recovery period after their workouts, and so do we. For a lot of us who are "hard chargers," this has to be developed. This is a component of high-level fitness programs that is often overlooked. As a result, people get injured and underperform. At The Performance Group, we encourage our clients to go hiking, get massage therapy, get extra rest, read, take time in a sensory float tank, do yoga, or meditate – whatever it takes – to create recovery periods and to restore energy.

Final Thoughts

In his book *Outliers*[59], Malcolm Gladwell tells us that what distinguishes successful people from average people is simple: *hard work*. There is no shortcut. We can create a new process to make change stick, but it is still hard work. Invite others into your process for support and encouragement, and your chances of long-term change are raised significantly.

Chapter takeaway: Once you have a breakthrough experience, take the time to create a routine and build the support network to make these changes stick. Don't let your achievement slip away. Don't just run toward the finish line, run through it.

---

59. Gladwell, M. (2008). *Outliers: The Story of Success.* New York, New York: Little Brown & Co.

Chapter 14

Optimize Your Operating System:
Giving Elite Performers Something More

> *"When talent, success, and opportunity aren't*
> *enough, we help you capture something more important."*

– Joel Landi

Capturing Something More

The topic of talent, success, and opportunity not being "enough" is an interesting one. From one perspective, our gaps in character sometimes prevent us from handling a lot of blessings well. From another perspective, no level of material reward will satisfy us if we feel that something is missing inside – and many of us have felt that. This chapter is about helping elite performers find what is missing and make the leap.

Elite professionals (athletes, entertainers) are often faced with sudden and previously unimaginable wealth. With it comes a host of temptations and pitfalls that have landed a percentage of these elite performers in court, jail, or the tabloids. Current examples of some well-known elite athletes and entertainers who have landed in this area include Aaron Hernandez, Adrian Peterson, Ray Rice, Oscar Pistorius, Bill Cosby, and Bruce Jenner.[60] [61]

Help Them Go Far

Elite athletes, entertainers, or anyone who has quickly inherited wealth are familiar with *going fast*. "If you want to go fast, go alone. If you want to go far, go together." This African proverb is a mantra for helping elites rewire destructive patterns of thinking that lead to unfulfilled personal lives. The solution is found in the proverb: instead of going fast, we can help them go far by helping them go together. One of the biggest clues to helping elites rewire what is missing is in their relationships. This is often a profound shift in trust, and it requires a clear roadmap to make it happen.

It Takes a Village and a Mentor

As the African proverb says, there are plenty of opportunities to go fast, but the key to going far – to having rewarding and sustainable success – is by going "together." Great coaching

60. Welter, C. (2014, September 29). NFL in Crisis – A Lack of Leadership in Raising Star Athletes. Retrieved May 5, 2015, from http://www.forbes.com/sites/johnkotter/2014/09/29/nfl-in-crisis-a-lack-of-leadership-in-raising-star-athletes/

61. Paul, M. (2014, December 18). Top 10 List of The Worst Reputations in Crisis For 2014. Retreived May 5, 2015, from http://reputationdoctor.com/2014/12/top-10-list-of-the-worst-reputations-in-crisis-for-2014/

provides the mentoring and the framework to achieve this goal. They need help to rewire *new* beliefs and values that will propel them beyond the rewards of their talent, which is often short lived. Some aspects of our approach include:

1. An accurate perspective on their performance, identity, and self-worth
2. A plan for personal development that is realistic and rewarding and includes (but is not limited to) targeted character development and building healthy relationships
3. A strategy to develop interests outside of their careers that are relevant and meaningful and serve to transition them successfully to their next opportunity

The Practical Steps

1. Face the real issue. Does the talent match the character? This is the elephant in the room. Most athletes/entertainers tend to spend more time on their body, athleticism and camera presence than their academic, relational and spiritual needs. We help fill in the gaps in these missing critical areas so that they can live balanced, rewarding, and productive lives off the field/stage as well. This includes building personal values, understanding intrinsic motive, and developing a mission statement.

2. Identify and avoid temptations, traps, and vices. We create a preemptive strike position that helps elite performers better assess their environment and create more positive outcomes.

3. Create a network of empowering relationships. When elites are underperforming at work, we examine their inner circle of relationships and create a network that is positive and goal oriented. We specifically address how to build proper connections within their organization and with their teammates and co-workers.

4. Build a healthy marriage and family. Building on the previous three steps, we solidify the cornerstone of their future, which is family. We accomplish it by clarifying their definitions and expectations, removing limiting beliefs, and identifying role models. We create a blueprint for how to live and maintain healthy marriage or family dynamics. We partner with religious leaders if desired.

5. Write a new narrative. The first four items above facilitate this. We recreate a mindset that removes limiting beliefs, installs liberating beliefs, and help elite performers to tell their life story through a lens that is authentic, hopeful and energizing.

6. Create a personal brand. We help elites create partner-ships outside the organization, become brand ambassadors, and make strategic public appearances. We also help them

with practicalities that connect them better to their public audience. It can also include an alliance with a charity or non-profit organization that has strategic relevance. We partner with industry standard leaders to facilitate this.

7. Discuss life after sports. This is a sobering and exciting discussion to have. When elites (especially athletes) are at the end of their career, we help construct their next opportunity. We offer a comprehensive approach to helping the elite clarify their greatest contribution outside of their current position. We accomplish this by doing an extensive assessment of gifts, strengths, experiences, and resources with industry standard tools, tests, and exercises. Follow-up opportunities may include rebranding within their current or previous profession, public speaking, TV or media, and becoming a brand ambassador or mentor. We partner with industry leaders to facilitate this.

What we do is completely confidential and designed to give our clients world-class service and care that caters to achieve an exceptional result. This is a collaborative effort, which may include key staff personnel within the organization and their talent agent. At The Performance Group, we hold their hand the whole way through this exciting yet demanding transition.

Chapter takeaway: The African proverb reminds us that our elite performers will need to build the right relationships to rise above the challenge of sudden wealth and its pitfalls. To go far, they must go together. We make that commitment. *Together, elites achieve more.*

Final Remarks

At the beginning of my coaching experience with each client, I show him or her a picture of Albert Einstein with the following quote below his face. "If you can't explain it simply, you don't understand it well enough." Coaching is simply about helping others. It's about drawing the best out of another person. It's about untangling the damaged and limiting thoughts and rewiring those thoughts with a version of an ideal self – not perfect – but ideal. It's about providing not only the tools and strategies, but also the key relationships for us to go further than we thought we could. I love being a catalyst for change in others. I love helping others take the necessary risks to fulfill their purpose. I love watching people's actions crush their fears and excuses. I love watching people conquer regret and remove it from their narrative.

Psychologist Brene Brown said in a TEDx Talk in Houston, July 2010, that it requires courage to tell your complete life story without shame or guilt. As my legacy, I want others to say about me that I helped them tell their story courageously. But more than that, I want to be remembered as a catalyst who helped others find fulfillment by powering up their relationships, performance, and purpose. That means capturing something more. That takes being *Rewired*.

45477390R00089

Made in the USA
Charleston, SC
23 August 2015